# HEARING GOD

Barry Bennett

Unless otherwise indicated, all Scripture quotations are taken from the King James Version of the Bible.



Published by Barry Bennett

Cover Design and Content Layout By: Catalyst Media

creatingcatalyst.com

Library of Congress Cataloging-in-Publication Data

ISBN: 978-194424321-0

Printed in the United States of America

# FOREWORD

God created everything by His words, and one word from God can totally change your life. The Lord never created anyone to fail. It is God's will for us all to prosper and fulfill a Divine plan for our lives. But it's impossible to do that without hearing from God. The reason so many people are frustrated and discouraged is because they have been trying to do their own thing. We have to have a word from God.

And the good news is that the Lord wants to speak to us more than we want to hear from Him. It's not God who isn't speaking. It's us who aren't listening properly.

In this book, Barry shares many times that he has heard from God with miraculous results, and he teaches you how to do the same. I see this working in Barry's life, and I know it will work for you too.

It is my pleasure to recommend Barry Bennett and his book, *Hearing God*. Barry is not a novice. He has been a missionary in Mexico and Chile for over twelve years. He directed a Spanish-speaking Bible school in Carrolton, Texas, before he and his wife, Betty Kay, came to work for me at Andrew Wommack Ministries.

Barry spent years answering all the doctrinal questions our ministry received, and he did it with excellence. We were constantly getting compliments on his answers and the spirit in which he gave them. Then one day he was a guest speaker in our Charis chapel hour. The students gave him a standing ovation, and they bought more of his CD's of that teaching than we had ever produced before. That's the first I knew of Barry as a speaker.

But what impressed me the most was his humility. He never promoted himself. As you will read in this book, he had a word from God that he would one day teach in our Charis Bible College, but he never tried to make that happen. He waited on God. That selflessness and confidence in a word from God is rare today. I was immediately drawn to that.

And Barry has proven to be a favorite instructor at Charis and an invaluable asset to the school precisely because of what he teaches in this book. Barry hears from God.

Do you feel like God has more for you than what you are experiencing? Are you ready to quit doing your own thing and follow God wherever He may lead you? Are you willing to leave mediocrity and boredom behind and embrace an abundant life? Then I know you are going to love this book.

Get ready for the greatest adventure you've ever had. The Lord's plans for you are greater than your plans for yourself. And as you learn how to hear and follow His voice, you are going to have the time of your life!

> *"… Did not our heart burn within us, as he talked with us by the way, and while he opened to us the scriptures?"*
>
> *Luke 24:32*

Andrew Wommack

# CONTENTS


| | |
|---|---|
| Foreword | v |
| Introduction | xiii |
| The Revelation of Righteousness | 1 |
| You Can Hear God | 7 |
| The Revelation of Jesus | 13 |
| The Revelation of God's Love | 19 |
| The Revelation of Protection | 25 |
| Revelation Knowledge | 31 |
| The Revelation of Healing | 37 |
| His Sheep Hear His Voice | 45 |
| A Revelation of the Future | 53 |

The Revelation of Words 63

He Will Guide You into All Truth 71

The Stirring of Your Spirit 79

The Secret Place 85

God Is Thinking About You! 93

Receiving Revelation 97

According to His Purpose 103

Final Thoughts 113

# INTRODUCTION

Many years ago, it became apparent to me that my faith in Jesus was not meant to be only a belief system or doctrinal statement. Many religions come complete with their beliefs and doctrines. Surely our faith and an understanding of God's love should include something more than a memorized set of rules.

I can remember the very first time I was aware of an answered prayer. I was in college and had missed a class in which an assignment was explained. I had no clue what was expected. I went to the campus library and sat in a study cubicle with no idea what to do next. I decided to talk to God. "Father, please send someone to me that is in my class and can explain the assignment to me."

This may not sound like much, but from a class of about 50 students in a school of 14,000 students, it seemed like a long shot. But in my simplistic way, I prayed. Less than one minute later a classmate walked by my cubicle, and

I stopped him and asked about the assignment. I was so excited! I'm sure he thought something was wrong with me. I got the information I needed, but I learned a lot more. God was real, He heard me and He cared enough to help me. That small incident revealed to me that my new faith was all about a relationship with God—one in which He would actually listen to me and communicate with me.

I wrote this book to encourage you to know that God wants to communicate with you. I am not talking about an audible voice but rather what I call "revelation knowledge." Everything about our faith in Jesus points to a loving relationship with the Father in which we can grow through this "revelation knowledge." Revelation knowledge is simply the communication of truth from God's Spirit to yours through various means. It is "hearing God."

As you read, you will become aware of three main points that I make repeatedly: 1) You were created with the ability to hear God, 2) Hearing God is the key to the abundant life in Christ, and 3) You should expect to hear God in your daily life.

I have tried to make it simple while hopefully stimulating you to expect your own relationship with the Father to grow and deepen.

## Chapter One

# THE REVELATION OF RIGHTEOUSNESS

I was lying face down on the living room floor of our small apartment in Corsicana, Texas. It was sometime in 1979, not long after returning from a four-month attempt at being missionaries in Mexico. My wife, Betty Kay, and I had only lasted four months for many reasons, the most important being that I had misunderstood God's leading. We had returned with almost nothing and needed some financial help from my parents to get on our feet again. I had a new job at a bank as the collections agent. My responsibilities included collecting on past due loans and repossessing cars. It was hardly what I had envisioned when we first set out to Mexico in August of 1978. What had happened?

I was feeling like a failure. Some of my friends from Bible College were having success in their missionary endeavors. They were making it. We had come home with 20 dollars to our names. In my mind I had failed. I had stepped out in faith (or presumption) and been unceremoniously deposited back in Texas with almost nothing.

As I was wallowing in my misery, a scripture exploded in my spirit. I had experienced something like this at other moments of my young Christian life, but this time seemed different.

> *For he hath made him to be sin for us, who knew no sin; that we might be made the righteousness of God in him.*
>
> *2 Corinthians 5:21*

I knew that scripture, but reached for my Bible to look it up. Yes, it said that we were made the righteousness of God in Christ! Instantly, I knew that I was righteous—as righteous as Jesus, as righteous as I would ever be. Something happened inside of me. What had been doctrinal understanding was transformed into revelation knowledge. I knew in my spirit that in spite of my failings and doubts, I was clean and pure in God's eyes. No matter what I had done to contribute to my own frustrations, I was loved. Nothing could change that!

From that moment on, I had a new understanding of redemption and of my identity in Christ. I can't say I understood the depths of what had just been revealed to my spirit. I can't say all of my doubts and fears left forever. But a fundamental truth had been revealed to me that would free me forever from guilt and self-condemnation. I might fail again, but nothing could ever change my true identity in Christ. I am righteous, free to stand in the presence of God as His child, free from guilt, condemnation and accusation. I could go on living with the spiritual understanding that regardless of my future ups and downs, I would always be who Jesus made me to be—a reflection of Himself.

That revelation has been the foundation for my many years of Christian growth and ministry. Time has only deepened the full understanding of what was revealed to my spirit that day in 1979. I had heard God, and hearing Him had transformed me. Though the knowledge of righteousness was not new to me, the spiritual revelation of it to my spirit man was new and powerful. What had been a doctrinal belief was now much more. Righteousness now meant something to me!

**What does it mean to reign in life?**

Righteousness is a gift that we receive by faith, and it also has very real benefits in this life. It empowers us to reign in life!

> *For if by one man's offence death reigned by one; much more they which receive abundance of grace and of the gift of righteousness* ***shall reign in life*** *by one, Jesus Christ.*
>
> *Romans 5:17*

What does it mean to reign in life? Just as sin, doubt, guilt and fear had reigned over me in the past, I was now in a position to live above those feelings and draw my identity from Jesus. Revelation knowledge had made this real to me.

> *The wicked flee when no one pursues, But* ***the righteous are bold as a lion.***
>
> *Prov. 28:1 NKJV (emphasis mine)*

Fear and timidity had marked my life for years. A fear of people, a fear of public speaking and a fear based on my own feelings of inadequacy and failures had set boundaries on my present and my future. But the revelation of righteousness opened the door to my true identity and potential.

Righteousness gives us the right to stand in and live in the presence of God without guilt or condemnation. It also gives us the authority to stand in the presence of sickness, corruption, and the works of the devil without fear. To the degree we understand the power of righteousness, we can prevail in every situation. Just as the sin of Adam and Eve released the destruction of the enemy into the earth, the righteousness of Jesus binds him. The enemy is powerless against the reborn, sinless nature of Christ in us! And what Jesus revealed to my spirit was that He had made me righteous! How did that revelation take place?

> *The Spirit Himself bears witness with our spirit that we are children of God.*
>
> *Romans 8:16 NKJV*

We are spiritual beings. All men have a spirit. When the Holy Spirit bears witness with our spirit of the true reality of who we are in Christ, we become more than conquerors. We can begin to "reign in life." The Spirit can bear witness with our spirit about anything that we have in Christ. That spiritual transaction can be called revelation knowledge or hearing God or seeing with our spiritual eyes.

Something equally as significant was revealed to me that day. Faith came by hearing! Doctrinal understanding became true revelation because the Spirit bore witness with my spirit. I suddenly had faith to see myself as never before. It wasn't an issue of willing myself to act stronger. It was the realization of who I really was in Him. It would be as if you had discovered that someone had deposited millions of dollars in your bank account. That "revelation" would change the way most of us act and think. That is what revelation knowledge can do for you. Something has been deposited in you through the new birth. The Holy Spirit wants to help you discover what is there!

**Faith came by hearing!**

As I have reflected on my Christian life that began in 1972, I have remembered other significant moments of "hearing" God and moments when faith was born. I realized the key to victorious living was to be found in the Spirit. When the Spirit bears witness with our spirit, something happens. Knowledge is transformed into revelation. Hope is transformed into faith. The impossible becomes possible.

Many years have passed since that life-changing moment. I could never have imagined I would be where I am today. I could easily say, "I never saw it coming." But one thing that has marked my journey for the past 40+ years is the reality of "revelation knowledge" or "hearing God." When the Spirit bears witness with our spirit, we move into another dimension of life: healing comes, direction comes, deliverance comes, and provision comes. But most importantly, faith comes.

## Chapter Two

# YOU CAN HEAR GOD

We have been created to hear God. We were created in His image with the capacity to hear His voice. Even after Adam sinned, he was still able to hear the voice of God as He walked in the Garden (Genesis 3:8-10). Though intimate communion was lost due to sin, and mankind entered into darkness, the capacity to hear God was not lost. God is seeking to communicate with every person on earth.

*I will hear what God the Lord will speak.*

*Psalm 85:8*

In the Scriptures, we find that there are two kinds of revelation available to mankind. There is general revelation, and there is specific revelation. General revelation is available to all men. General revelation can be seen in creation and demonstrates there is a God.

*The heavens declare the glory of God, and the sky above proclaims his handiwork. Day to day pours out speech, and night to night reveals knowledge. There is no speech, nor are there words, whose voice is not heard. Their voice goes out through all the earth, and their words to the end of the world.*

*Psalm 19:1-4 ESV*

In other words, creation itself is a manifestation of God's Word and is continually "speaking" to humanity. Paul said it this way:

*Because what may be known of God is manifest in them, for God has shown it to them. For since the creation of the world His invisible attributes are clearly seen, being understood by the things that are made, even His eternal power and Godhead, so that they are without excuse.*

*Romans 1:19-20 NKJV*

This is exciting and troubling at the same time. It is God's grace that gives every man the opportunity to hear Him and to know He exists. All of creation testifies that there is a Creator and that life came from Him. It is man's great loss that he often seeks meaning and purpose in life through the things created rather than in the Creator.

Because of the sin, darkness, and corruption in the world, most people follow one of two paths in life. Many choose to live for the flesh. That means they choose to satisfy every desire and whim in the search for meaning and identity through the lust of the flesh and the eyes. Others choose to seek after a God they do not know and create religions that will attempt to understand and satisfy the deity they have imagined. This can include great personal sacrifice and even self-abuse. As we look at the world in which we live, we can see both groups seeking for meaning either from self-indulgence or from a religious structure they must follow. The apostle Paul declares that all mankind knew God, meaning creation reveals Him, but they chose to go after other things.

> *Because that, when they knew God, they glorified him not as God, neither were thankful; but became vain in their imaginations, and their foolish heart was darkened.*
>
> *Romans 1:21*

Jesus mentioned this same problem with the Jews to whom He had come to reveal God. Although they had the Scriptures, many had fallen into observing the rules rather than seeking a relationship with God.

> *For the hearts of this people have grown dull. Their ears are hard of hearing, And their eyes they have closed, Lest they should see with their eyes and hear with their ears, Lest they should understand with their hearts and turn, So that I should heal them.*
>
> *Matthew 13:15 NKJV*

Notice that they had closed their eyes and they had allowed their ears to become dull. It isn't that God had stopped speaking; it is that most of them were so preoccupied with the issues of life, they gave little time or attention to hearing Him. And yet, they were created to hear Him and to live by every word that proceeds from His mouth! And so are we today.

> *It is written, Man shall not live by bread alone, but by every word that proceedeth out of the mouth of God.* God is still speaking.
>
> *Matthew 4:4*

While general revelation is the revelation of God's existence to all mankind, specific revelation is the direct communication of God to our spirit man.

All men are spiritual beings created in the image of God, and all men have the capacity to "hear" Him. All men have spirits—even fallen, lost men. It is the spirit of man that must be born again and come into union with God. But even apart from that union, the reality exists that all men can hear God. The Spirit of God can communicate with the spirit of man even though man is lost.

**God wants to communicate with you!**

The darkness of sin has not silenced God, but it has certainly diverted our attention away from Him. God desires to communicate with us through creation, through His written Word, through prophets and preachers, and even through the circumstances of life. As Paul said in Romans, men are without excuse (Romans 1:20).

There is an even deeper dimension of "hearing" available to believers, to those who have been born again by the Spirit of God.

> *For what man knows the things of a man except the spirit of the man which is in him? Even so no one knows the things of God except the Spirit of God.*

> *Now we have received, not the spirit of the world, but the Spirit who is from God, that we might know the things that have been freely given to us by God.*
>
> *1 Corinthians 2:11–12 NKJV*

God wants to communicate with you! He wants to show you all that has become yours through Christ. He wants to bring you out of despair, discouragement, fear, sickness and poverty into the abundant life. This goes beyond the general revelation of Himself that is available to all through creation. This is the specific revelation to our re-created spirits that we might know the greatness of our inheritance in Him! God wants to teach you, give you wisdom, prepare you, warn you and deliver you. He is speaking! Why aren't many hearing?

> *But the natural man receiveth not the things of the Spirit of God: for they are foolishness unto him: neither can he know them, because they are spiritually discerned.*
>
> *1 Corinthians 2:14*

Sadly, many Christians could be classified as "natural" men, not because they aren't born again, but because they simply give no time to the things of God. The cares of this world have choked the Word, and they have chosen to live as natural men, not spiritual. Even though their spirits are alive to God and His voice, they seldom hear or recognize His promptings because they haven't taken the time to prepare their hearts to hear Him.

Consider the challenge of the blind and the deaf. In the natural world, they are certainly at a disadvantage. Those sights and sounds that most take for granted are unknown to those who cannot see or hear. It is a different life that they live. Adjustments are made, but the rich world of sight and sound remains locked away and only imagined.

The natural man is living a similar life. A life without hearing God is a minimal existence at best. We were created to hear Him. Choosing to ignore Him and live life on the natural level is similar to being blind and deaf at the same time. You can adjust, but you will never know the abundant life. We were created to live in communion with the Father, and His abundance, favor, blessing, wisdom and instruction are available to us. Abundant life begins with a desire to hear Him.

> *The hearing ear, and the seeing eye, the Lord hath made even both of them.*
>
> *Proverbs 20:12*

Chapter Three

# THE REVELATION OF JESUS

One of the most important passages that deals with the subject of revelation knowledge and hearing God is found in Matthew, chapter 16.

> *He said to them, "But who do you say that I am?" Simon Peter answered and said, "You are the Christ, the Son of the living God." Jesus answered and said to him, "Blessed are you, Simon Bar-Jonah,* ***for flesh and blood has not revealed this to you, but My Father who is in heaven****.*
>
> *Matthew 16:15-17 NKJV (emphasis mine)*

Peter's response to Jesus' question was not based on logic or classroom learning. God had revealed Jesus' true identity to Peter, and that revelation was to be the foundation for His church. Though Peter had his ups and downs in his walk with God, the foundation of his life was established on a revelation. Something was quickened to his spirit, and because it was a revelation, hell could not prevail against it. (See verses 18 and 19.)

Without a doubt, the most important revelation for anyone to have is of the identity of Jesus. Until we have spiritual knowledge of the identity of Jesus Christ, it will be difficult for other revelations to find a place in our lives. Peter's declaration and Jesus' response were no small thing. The entire church and the authority of the church can only exist to the degree we know who Jesus is.

After Jesus' resurrection, He found two disciples walking down a road and joined them to discuss the recent events of His crucifixion. However, the two disciples didn't recognize Jesus. They were too distraught over His death to see that He was walking with them! Later, they sat down to eat together.

> *Now it came to pass, as He sat at the table with them, that He took bread, blessed and broke it, and gave it to them.* ***Then their eyes were opened*** *and they knew Him; and He vanished from their sight. And they said to one another,* ***"Did not our heart burn within us*** *while He talked with us on the road, and while He opened the Scriptures to us?"*
>
> *Luke 24:30–32 NKJV (emphasis mine)*

Most likely, these disciples were in the presence of Jesus for several hours (Luke 24:15-32), but their eyes were closed to His true identity. However, there came a moment in which their eyes were opened, and they knew Him! Jesus hadn't changed. It had been Jesus the whole time, and they even remembered that His sharing of scripture with them had caused their hearts to "burn"

Levels of revelation as we grow.



within them. But even so, their eyes were closed to His identity. How often is God speaking to us, and we don't even know it?

The great need in the world today is for people to have a revelation of Jesus Christ. God is not withholding that knowledge from anyone, but only those hearts that are open to such knowledge will find it.

Revelation knowledge can be described as the opening of our spiritual eyes to see or the opening of our spiritual ears to hear and understand spiritual truths. Didn't Jesus come to do precisely that?

> *The Spirit of the Lord is upon me, because he hath anointed me to preach the gospel to the poor; he hath sent me to heal the brokenhearted, to preach deliverance to the captives,* ***and recovering of sight to the blind,*** *to set at liberty them that are bruised.*
>
> *Luke 4:18 (emphasis mine)*

Certainly this includes physical sight to the physically blind, but it also speaks of spiritual sight (revelation knowledge) to those who had been in darkness. Consider Jesus' words to Paul when he was called into the ministry. Jesus is telling Paul what the purpose of his ministry will be.

> ***To open their eyes,*** *and to turn them from darkness to light, and from the power of Satan unto God, that they may receive forgiveness of sins, and inheritance among them which are sanctified by faith that is in me.*
>
> *Acts 26:18 (emphasis mine)*

Notice that being delivered from the power of Satan, receiving forgiveness of sin and receiving our inheritance in Christ all depends on having our eyes opened! This opening of the eyes is "revelation knowledge" or "the Spirit bearing witness with our spirit." This is why Jesus asked Peter who He was and told him such knowledge did not come from man but from God. Then Jesus declared to Peter that such a revelation came complete with the keys of the kingdom!

Authority comes from revelation knowledge.

> *And I will give unto thee the keys of the kingdom of heaven: and whatsoever thou shalt bind on earth shall be bound in heaven: and whatsoever thou shalt loose on earth shall be loosed in heaven.*
>
> *Matthew 16:19*

**Authority comes from revelation knowledge.** What the Spirit of God reveals to our spirit gives birth to authority in our lives. Mental understanding, while valuable, isn't enough. We were created to receive from God on a spiritual level.

As I compared my own experiences of hearing God with these passages, I realized the truths of God, which are quickened to our spirit (things which we "see" and "hear" on the inside), represent the foundation on which the rest of our lives are built. Not only can such revelation not be shaken, there is a spiritual authority that accompanies it and gives us power in this life.

When the realities of righteousness were quickened

to my spirit, the promises of righteousness became mine to receive and enjoy. What other things did God want to reveal to me?

> *I... will reveal unto them the abundance of peace and truth.*
>
> *Jeremiah 33:6*

Chapter Four

# THE REVELATION OF GOD'S LOVE

All of us have experienced rejection. Rejection is a powerful weapon against our self-worth. Rejection can breed thoughts of inadequacy, hopelessness, anger, bitterness, fear and depression. Whether the rejection has been on the playground at school, from a romantic interest, from a potential employer or from parents, rejection can cause great damage in how we see ourselves and our value to others.

Rejection is the soil in which unbelief grows. Each time we experience rejection, the potential for doubt and unbelief increases. How can you have faith in life, others or yourself when you believe you are unlovely, incapable or inadequate in some way? The seeds of rejection produce the harvest of failure. Our identity becomes tied to the rejections we have experienced, and we set our expectations in life according to the memory of the rejections we carry in our hearts. This is nothing more than bondage and oppression.

This same attitude we often carry into our relationship with God. If others don't like us, why would God? As a result, it is difficult, if not impossible, to enjoy a loving, trusting relationship with the Father. If He sees all of our faults and is more aware of all of our weaknesses than anyone else, why should we expect anything good from Him?

Listen to this:

> *To the praise of the glory of His grace, by which He made us accepted in the Beloved.*
>
> *Ephesians 1:6 NKJV*

Are there words that can describe what Paul just said? Let's look at the context in the previous verses.

> *Blessed be the God and Father of our Lord Jesus Christ, who has blessed us with every spiritual blessing in the heavenly places in Christ, just as He chose us in Him before the foundation of the world, that we should be holy and without blame before Him in love, having predestined us to adoption as sons by Jesus Christ to Himself, according to the good pleasure of His will, to the praise of the glory of His grace, by which He has made us accepted in the Beloved.*
>
> *Ephesians 1:3-6 NKJV*

In this passage, Paul declares that God has blessed us (v. 3). He has chosen us to be without blame before Him in love (v. 4). He has predetermined that we are sons and daughters in His family—not slaves or orphans (v. 5). By grace, He has made us accepted! (v. 6) This is the nearly too good to be true Good News!

The Greek meaning of the word "accepted" means more than our understanding of the English word. It means "to make graceful, charming, lovely, agreeable, to surround with favor and to honor with blessings." Wow! Do you see yourself as agreeable to God and surrounded with favor and blessings? Most of us need a revelation to see that.

Something I understood mentally had been made real to my spirit man by the Spirit of God. This revelation of God's love and acceptance wasn't even an area in which I thought I needed help. I understood God loved me from day one of my salvation. The later revelation of righteousness only served to make me more secure in my identity in Christ. I didn't think anything was missing.

But in the past few years, and even quite recently, the Spirit of God has touched me, and I "saw" His love like I never had before. The love of God is not just a doctrinal statement, but it is actually His infinite desire to see me prosper on every level of life—spirit, soul and body. I saw Him focused on me in a personal way. I can't explain it other than to say that it changed me.

Do you see yourself as God's favorite? Not just another redeemed person in the sea of humanity that covers all people from the time of creation, but His favorite? You would probably agree that God loves you, but do you believe He likes you?

I know it sounds egotistical and perhaps even sacrilegious, but I have come to believe that unless you can see yourself as the object of God's love and that He would have sent Jesus to die for you and you alone, you really won't enjoy the full expression of the abundant life.

How would you live your life differently if you knew you were the only object of God's love and grace? How would it impact you if you knew all of His power was at your disposal? What would you do differently when you discovered He had given you the keys of the Kingdom and every good gift? How would you feel to learn that all of the angels of heaven existed to minister for you?

I suspect your attitude toward yourself and toward life might change. Your posture might change. Your vision for life might be different. The way you treat others would reflect the love you had received from God as His favorite. Your words would change. You would think and speak differently. You would be an ambassador of Almighty God and an expression of His love.

His compassion would be your compassion. His mercy would be your mercy. His heart for others would be your heart for others. You would have no fear because it would have been replaced with absolute confidence in your Father's love. You would have total peace and confidence knowing that you are God's child!

Can you imagine that? You should try, because it is all true.

> *The Lord your God is in your midst, a Mighty One, who will save. He will rejoice over you with gladness, He will renew you with His love, He will rejoice over you with singing.*
>
> *Zephaniah 3:17 MEV*

Before you were ever conceived, God knew you and chose to love and accept you. You may have been picked last on the playground, but you are first in the heart of God. You may not have Hollywood looks, but you couldn't look any better to God. You are unique. There is no one like you. You have divine potential and a divine purpose in this world. You are accepted!

> **Ask Him to reveal His love to you.**

If you can get your heart wrapped around this, faith will spring forth. When we know there is no chance of rejection, we can believe the promises, enjoy His fellowship, see our potential and have peace.

Only the Spirit of God can reveal this to you. It can happen in an instant. Ask Him to reveal His love to you. Paul prayed this way for the Ephesian believers.

> *...that ye, being rooted and grounded in love, May be able to comprehend with all saints what is the breadth, and length, and depth, and height; And to know the love of Christ, which passeth knowledge, that ye might be filled with all the fulness of God.*
>
> *Ephesians 3:17-19*

How can you know something that passes knowledge? Revelation knowledge! And Paul goes on to pray *"that you might be filled with all the fulness of God."* Filled with all of God? I don't know if this is hitting you like it hit me, but Christ in us, the hope of glory, is far beyond a doctrine. God lives in us. Christ lives in us. The Spirit lives in us (these three are One), and their riches are unsearchable, their love past knowing and their fullness in us is incomprehensible to our natural minds.

And that is the gospel message. God wants to live in you and bless you. On this "rock" of revelation, God will build His life in you, and nothing shall prevail against it!

> *I have loved thee with an everlasting love: therefore with loving kindness have I drawn thee.*
>
> *Jeremiah 31:3*

## Chapter Five

# THE REVELATION OF PROTECTION

It was early in the morning, a few miles outside of Port Au Prince, Haiti, in the summer of 1987. I had been asked to accompany my senior pastor and the mission's pastor on a week-long, fact-finding trip to a Haitian orphanage. The missionary in charge was looking for a church or an organization to take over as he planned to retire soon. We had landed the night before and been greeted by chaos in the city, burning piles of tires, damaged cars, and people moving in groups through the dark streets.

We asked what was going on, to which our host replied, "The people are just celebrating." I thought to myself, "I'm glad that my car or house isn't involved in this celebration. Too much celebrating could be dangerous!" It wasn't until we reached the orphanage compound outside of the city that the missionary told us the complete story.

The people were rioting due to the unstable political and economic climate in the country. According to our host, the city was going to be shut down by the people, and all traffic and commerce would come to a halt at various times during the next few days. Violence was common in these situations. We would have to be very careful in our movements if we decided to go into the city.

With that in mind, we were given our rooms for the night. The following morning, I got up with my Bible and climbed the outside stairs to the flat roof of the mission's house. From there, I could see the ocean and some of the surrounding homes and businesses. All seemed peaceful. But the Lord knew of the potential for danger, and as I read my Bible, I came to the following scripture.

> *Blessed be the Lord, For He has made marvelous His lovingkindness to me in a* ***besieged*** *city.*
>
> *Psalm 31:21 NASB (emphasis mine)*

At that moment, faith was born. This word came alive in my heart, and I knew that, regardless of the circumstances, God would deliver me if I needed delivering. I instantly had peace.

I was growing in my sensitivity to the Spirit. I was learning to "hear" God. Very often, the Lord speaks to me through His Word. I can't count how many times the Lord has given me promises, direction and specific revelation for my life and circumstances as I was reading the Word. It is the primary way that God deals with me. My time of prayer and reading that morning prepared me for the adventures ahead. But what if I hadn't been reading and praying? Would I have had the same faith for the rest of the trip? Would fear have opened the door to the enemy?

Paul was in a place of prayer when he received the following warning from God:

> *And it came to pass, that, when I was come again to Jerusalem, even while I prayed in the temple, I was in a trance; And saw him saying unto me, Make haste, and get thee quickly out of Jerusalem: for they will not receive thy testimony concerning me.*
>
> *Acts 22:17-18*

Make haste, and get thee quickly out of Jerusalem! What if Paul had decided to skip his prayer time and go to a coffee shop instead? How would things have been different for him that day and perhaps for the rest of his life? Is it possible that we have missed some of God's warnings and instructions simply because we were too preoccupied to hear Him?

God wants to reveal things to us. He wants to show us things to come.

> *Howbeit when he, the Spirit of truth, is come, he will guide you into all truth: for he shall not speak of himself; but whatsoever he shall hear, that shall he speak: and he will shew you* ***things to come.***
>
> *John 16:13 (emphasis mine)*

Once again, the Spirit will bear witness with our spirit. He not only teaches us (as He taught me about righteousness), He warns us, comforts us, directs us, corrects us and delivers us. But we must be sensitive to Him.

Our days in Haiti were adventurous to say the least. We did travel to Port Au Prince for the few hours that the city was declared to be open. We saw the incredible poverty and the human misery that spiritual darkness produces. I witnessed a man chasing a former secret police officer with a hatchet as I browsed in the main market. They passed inches away from me. I have no idea of the outcome, but to see such violence in the broad daylight was startling. But I had a word from God.

Our bus ride back to the compound was interrupted when the driver decided it was too dangerous to continue the trip and ordered everyone off the bus. We walked to a nearby gas station that was teeming with a hundred or more Haitian men. They instantly gathered around us and wanted to talk. We never felt threatened, but it wasn't the most comfortable situation. We heard gunshots not far away.

A large truck came down the road, and the crowd of men ran into the highway to stop the truck. They made the driver get out and open the back of the truck. It was then we realized that these men were hijacking trucks and stealing the cargo. This truck was empty, and the driver and the men had a big laugh. As the truck pulled away, all of the men came back and gathered around our little group. We were feeling a little different about things now. The missionary was able to pay a man to drive us the rest of the way in his car, and we were able to get back to the compound safely.

That night, it was announced on the radio by the opposition forces that the country would be shut down indefinitely early the next morning. We decided that we needed to make it to the airport as quickly as possible, and hopefully get our tickets changed to the earliest departing flight. Things were getting interesting, but I had a word from God. *He has made marvelous His loving kindness to me in a besieged city.* A word from God will put you over when things seem negative. I already knew in my heart that I was safe. I knew that no matter what happened I would be delivered.

I won't take the time to relate all of the details of the next few hours. There was a late night, headlights-off dash into the city through the back streets, avoiding barricades, to a one-star hotel, which was filled with others like us who each had their own story to tell. Bus windows and car windows had been smashed, people had been roughed up and the general environment was deteriorating quickly.

We tried to sleep for a couple of hours before making another trip, this time by bus, to the airport. There we encountered hundreds of people sleeping on the sidewalks and in the lobby. Lines were forming hours ahead of time for the flights that were scheduled that day. Our tickets were for two days later, and all I could see was a mass of scared humanity—all wanting to board the same airplanes. *But I had a word from God.*

After hours of waiting, negotiating and believing, we were given standby tickets for what turned out to be the last plane that left the country for five days. And after what seemed like thousands getting on the plane before us, including the airport workers, our names were finally called. I believe we were the last three to board. God had shown me His loving kindness in a besieged city. How much did His protection depend upon me hearing Him? If fear had entered my heart, would the outcome have been the same?

**We need to be continually quickened by God's Word.**

A scripture quickened to your spirit at the opportune time can change your destiny. Oftentimes, we find ourselves in the midst of trials and adverse circumstances. It is during these times that the Word quickened to our spirits can deliver us, give us wisdom, direction, authority and faith.

> *Incline your ear, and come unto me: hear, and your soul shall live.*
>
> *Isaiah 55:3*

Revelation knowledge doesn't only deal with major doctrinal truths and great mysteries, but also with the daily affairs of life. We need to be continually quickened by God's Word.

> *Deliver me according to thy word.*
>
> *Psalm 119:170*

## Chapter Six

# REVELATION KNOWLEDGE

The world might call it intuition. Some would say it is a sixth sense. Perhaps in the realm of human experience there are such things. But in the realm of the Spirit-filled life, we are called into a far deeper communion in which the things of God can be revealed to us. One purpose of the Spirit of God in our lives is *that we might know* the things He has given us.

> *Now we have received, not the spirit of the world, but the spirit which is of God; that we might know the things that are freely given to us of God.*
>
> *1 Corinthians 2:12*

Revelation knowledge is the key to faith and victory in the Christian life. It is the foundation for the overcoming life!

There are two kinds of knowledge in the world: natural knowledge and spiritual knowledge. Most of what we live by is natural in nature; even Bible knowledge can be accumulated with no real impact on our lives. We know what we believe with our minds, but many times what we believe does not manifest the way we think that it should.

Paul touched on this in his writings. There are different levels of understanding, which Paul mentions in 1 Corinthians.

> *What shall I profit you, except I shall speak to you either by* ***revelation****, or by* ***knowledge****, or by* ***prophesying****, or by* ***doctrine?***
>
> *1 Corinthians 14:6 (emphasis mine)*

He speaks of: 1) Doctrine - something that can be learned, 2) Prophecy - words that can inspire/edify/exhort/comfort, 3) Knowledge - something we understand well enough to teach to others, and 4) Revelation - that which transforms us.

## Many have good doctrine but live frustrated lives.

While doctrine and knowledge are incredibly important, they may not produce the change that is needed. Many have good doctrine but live frustrated lives.

Paul himself learned the gospel–not from men but by revelation.

> *For I neither received it of man, neither was I taught it, but by the revelation of Jesus Christ.*
>
> *Galatians 1:12*

Paul's energy, faith and dedication to the gospel and the call of God on his life were due to the life-changing revelation he received from Jesus. The Spirit of God revealed the things of God to the spirit of Paul.

The Spirit can reveal anything to our spirit, and that revelation becomes a part of us. "But he that is joined unto the Lord is one spirit." (1 Corinthians 6:17) Since we are one spirit with Him, it is simply a matter of His Spirit quickening our spirit to the realities of who we are and of our needs being met in Him.

Revelation knowledge or hearing God is spiritual in nature and not easy to nail down. You know it when you know it. It goes beyond the intellect and the emotions into the realm of spiritual vision and understanding.

> *While we look not at the things which are seen, but at the things which are not seen: for the things which are seen are temporal; but the things which are not seen are eternal.*
>
> *2 Corinthians 4:18*

Revelation knowledge transcends human intellect and the tangible world of the visible. It is the birth place for true faith.

**How does revelation come?** Obviously it comes from God, but it is not something that God is withholding. It would seem more like we are too distracted to seek it with our whole hearts. Paul prayed for the Ephesians that God would give them a spirit of revelation. We should pray that same way.

> *That the God of our Lord Jesus Christ, the Father of glory, may give unto you the spirit of wisdom and* ***revelation in the knowledge of him:*** *The* ***eyes of your understanding being enlightened;*** *that ye may know what is the hope of his calling.*
>
> *Ephesians 1:17–18 (emphasis mine)*

Paul prayed for the Christians in this way because such revelation and enlightenment is not automatic the moment you receive salvation. If it were, all believers would be walking in the same realm of peace, love and victory. There would be no failure or lack in our lives. But as we look at the believers around us and at our own lives, we must be honest and realize that revelation knowledge is lacking.

This "revelation" takes us into a different dimension of understanding His power toward us who believe. That is the secret of power—revelation! Many are born again and baptized in the Spirit but still seem to lack power in their lives. Why? Spiritual revelation has yet to be quickened to them. The eyes of their understanding have yet to be enlightened.

**Revelation knowledge comes as we create the right environment for it by spending time in the Word and in prayer, praise and meditation.** We will "see" healing. We will "see" our authority. We will "hear" the Spirit. Mental knowledge will become spiritual revelation, and the victorious life will become a reality.

Revelation knowledge will prompt our faith to

proclaim what we know to be true. When we speak to our bodies, it won't be a formula confession but rather a powerful agreement with what we have received by revelation. There is a difference between the doctrine of "by His stripes I am healed," and the revelation of that same truth. One you can teach. The other you release through faith-filled words because it has been quickened to you by the Spirit.

Living in the reality of our re-born spirit is a product of truly knowing by revelation what is in us through Jesus. You will know when it happens. As you meditate and pray the scripture mentioned above, God will show you what is "the hope of His calling."

Make this your prayer:

"Father, I thank you that it is your desire that I have a spirit of revelation into the things of the kingdom and a true enlightened understanding of your power toward me. Thank you for revealing these things to my spirit." (from Ephesians 1:17-19)

The heart of a believer should be a heart that desires true fellowship with the Father. Such fellowship will produce the revelation that Paul speaks of. When we knock, ask and seek, things are revealed to us.

Only by revelation knowledge can we truly know the nature of God within us and all that He has deposited into our re-born spirits. Head knowledge is not enough.

*For this cause we also, since the day we heard it, do not cease to pray for you, and to desire that ye might be filled with the knowledge of his will in all wisdom and* ***spiritual understanding.***

*Colossians 1:9 (emphasis mine)*

## Chapter Seven

# THE REVELATION OF HEALING

We had traveled to a remote mountain village in Guatemala to share with a group of Christians and witness a baptism service. It was 1989, and we had been in Guatemala for about 7 months studying Spanish. This was an opportunity to meet with indigenous people and share our faith. After the baptism, we were invited to eat an afternoon meal in very rustic accommodations and poor sanitary conditions. It was probably during the meal that I ate something contaminated.

Not many days later, I began to feel weak and nauseated. This continued for a few days until one morning when I woke up and looked in the mirror. Yellow eyes and skin were looking back at me. A trip to a Christian doctor confirmed that I had hepatitis. After the required blood work, the doctor told me I would be in bed for four months. Since we had plans to move to

Chile before that time period would end, the four-month verdict was not welcome.

Once alone in bed, I quickly began to remind God of all the reasons I shouldn't be sick. I was a Bible college graduate and a missionary for Him! I was following the call of God on my life! I shouldn't be sick! I believed in healing! But all of those good things weren't enough. I needed something deeper.

I spent my days in the Word, reading faith-filled books and listening to teaching tapes. I probably became more focused on the Word than I had ever been. There was nothing else to do! What I didn't realize at the time was that I was creating an environment to hear God.

In spite of my calling, background and endeavors for the Lord, I can see now that hearing Him was not a daily priority. My time in bed gave me the opportunity to eliminate all distractions and focus on hearing Him.

> *And great multitudes came together to hear, and to be healed by him of their infirmities.*
>
> *Luke 5:15*

After four weeks, it happened. I had weakly shuffled out of my little bedroom and was sitting in our common living/eating area. The family was off to the market, and I had the house to myself. While sitting in a simple, wooden chair, the Spirit of God spoke to me. *"By my stripes you were healed."* I knew that scripture. I could teach healing. I had read that scripture and others about healing. I was not a doubter about God's will. But suddenly, what had been doctrine became life! The Spirit bore witness with my spirit. I knew I was healed!

I got dressed and took a walk down the street. Healed people can do that. I still looked gaunt and yellow, but something was different. I knew that I knew that I knew that I was healed. The Word of the Lord had come to me.

I quickly began to recover and regain weight. The four month prognosis had transformed into four weeks because I was able to hear God. What did I learn?

First of all, God was not testing me. Sickness is never His will. Secondly, God's Word is always alive and active. The verse that was quickened to my spirit didn't suddenly come alive that day in 1989. *It has always been alive!* It was me who was living on auto pilot and not creating an environment to hear God. I was not living by every word that proceeds from the mouth of God. Therefore, when the time to receive healing came around, I wasn't in a place to hear Him. It took me four weeks to get to that place.

The revelation of an already known truth brought faith and healing. It is from that experience that I realized just knowing about something, even knowing it well enough to teach it, wasn't enough. Truth is spiritual. It must be quickened in our re-born spirit in order for faith to be born and changes to occur. We must learn to "hear" and "see" with spiritual ears and eyes.

Jesus said it this way concerning the Jews of His day:

*For the hearts of this people have grown dull. Their ears are hard of hearing, And their eyes they have closed, Lest they should see with their eyes and hear with their ears, Lest they should understand with their hearts and turn, So that I should heal them.*

*Matthew 13:15 NKJV*

In this verse, Jesus explains exactly why some do not receive healing. It is a heart issue. The heart has become consumed with the worries of life. Spiritual ears are dull. Spiritual vision is clouded. A heart that is out of tune with the Spirit of God has difficulty in hearing. Faith is blocked.

Sadly, in many churches, these believers are instructed to trust in the sovereignty of God and accept the fact that He was in control of these events. Rather than learning to grow in sensitivity to the Spirit of God, we often create theological excuses. Once again, it is not simply a doctrine or a belief system that heals us and relieves suffering. It is a fruit of hearing God. It is in our times of communion with the Father that His Word is quickened to our spirits.

Consider the following examples of revelation knowledge and how healing flowed.

**Blind Bartimaeus had a revelation of Jesus' identity:** *"Jesus, thou son of David, have mercy on me."* (Mark 10:47) In some way Bartimaeus received a revelation of Jesus' identity as the Son of David. To the Jews, this was a title of the Messiah, the One who would come and heal and deliver the oppressed. This revelation caused Jesus to stop and minister to Bartimaeus, and he received his sight.

**The Centurion had a revelation of Jesus' authority:** *"But speak the word only and my servant shall be healed. For I am a man under authority..."* (Matthew 8:8-9). The Centurion didn't ask Jesus to come to his house. He knew that Jesus' words were enough. He understood spiritual authority! What is interesting is that the Centurion was not a Jew, and yet the Spirit of God had revealed something to him. The healing of his servant was the result. Jesus declared that He hadn't found such great faith in all of Israel! Revelation knowledge gave birth to great faith!

**The friends of the man on the stretcher had a revelation of the power of Jesus' presence:** *"And the power of the Lord was present to heal them....and they sought means to bring him in and to lay him before him."* (Luke 5:17-18) Something inspired these men to press on when the natural circumstances were against them. Faith was born in their hearts, and they were able to climb up to the roof and make a hole through which they lowered their friend. What prompted such faith and perseverance?

**The two blind men had a revelation of His mercy and compassion:** *"And, behold, two blind men sitting by the way side, when they heard that Jesus passed by, cried out, saying, Have mercy on us, O Lord, thou Son of David....So Jesus had compassion on them, and touched their eyes: and immediately their eyes received sight, and they followed him."* (Matthew 20:30-34) Not only did these two blind men have a revelation of Jesus' identity, they understood that the Son of David was a man of miraculous compassion. That revelation opened the door for their healing.

**The woman with the issue of blood had a revelation of Jesus' anointing:** *"When she had heard of Jesus, [she] came in the press behind, and touched his garment. For she said, If I may touch but his clothes, I shall be whole."* (Mark 5:27-28) Though this woman was "unclean" by Jewish law, she had a revelation that even Jesus' clothes carried His anointing. That revelation propelled her into the crowd, and she pressed on until she was able to touch His garment.

**Hearing Him is a key to healing in our bodies.**

What is striking to me is that in each of these cases ordinary people were motivated by a revelation of what God had made available. These were not theological scholars, and I doubt that they were even diligent seekers of God. But their hearts were not hardened, and their ears were not dull. They heard the Spirit of God—not because they were special, but because they were open. Faith was born in their hearts and actions followed.

Hearing Him is a key to healing in our bodies. Too often we look to others for our healing. We feel out of touch with God and unworthy. We are far too aware that our relationship with God isn't what it could be.

But stop and think about it. No one in the gospels had a close relationship with God. They weren't even born again! And yet, all who approached Jesus got healed. How can that be? They simply "saw" some aspect of His nature in their spirit, which generated faith. It wasn't that they were mature or even devoted to God. They just got a glimpse of His identity or His authority or His compassion or His anointing or power, and that simple revelation brought them to Him with expectancy.

That should be encouraging to us! There are no hoops to jump through. All we need is to be open to "seeing" and “hearing” the nature of God and receiving what is ours.

> *A great multitude of people out of all Judaea and Jerusalem…came to hear him, and to be healed of their diseases.*
>
> *Luke 6:17*

## Chapter Eight

# HIS SHEEP HEAR HIS VOICE

Hearing God is not only a possibility, it is a necessity. Relationship is a fruit of communion. Both parties in a relationship are responsible for communicating. Both parties have things to say and hear. This kind of communion with the Father was the foundation for Jesus' ministry. How can we expect to do more with less?

> *And in the morning, rising up a great while before day, he went out, and departed into a solitary place, and there prayed.*
>
> *Mark 1:35*

Have you ever asked yourself why Jesus prayed? I mean, He is Jesus, the Word made flesh. Why would He pray? Is it possible that Jesus needed to pray in order to hear the Father? Did Jesus need undistracted moments in which to hear God and receive revelation for His ministry?

> *Then Jesus answered and said to them, "Most assuredly, I say to you, the Son can do nothing of Himself, but what He sees the Father do; for whatever He does, the Son also does in like manner. For the Father loves the Son, and shows Him all things that He Himself does."*
>
> *John 5:19-20 NKJV*

The vision, direction and faith for Jesus' ministry were born in His times of prayer and communion with the Father. He goes so far as to say that He could do nothing of Himself! That may seem hard for us to comprehend, but His ability to heal, cast out demons, still storms, multiply food and raise the dead was a result of "hearing" the Father or "seeing" what the Father was doing. It was revelation knowledge.

Jesus declared that we would also be limited to our relationship with Him.

> *He that abideth in me, and I in him, the same bringeth forth much fruit: for without me ye can do nothing.*
>
> *John 15:5*

It should come as no surprise that we are working with the same resources Jesus had. He could only do what He received from the Father, and we can only bring forth the fruit of redemption if we abide in Him. Our Christian life is not all mental. If hearing the Father was so vitally important to Jesus, shouldn't it be important to us as well?

Jesus said, *"My sheep hear my voice, and I know them, and they follow me."* (John 10:27) This kind of hearing is revelation. This kind of seeing is revelation. It is the Spirit bearing witness with our spirit. **The quickening of the Word to our inner man produces spiritual understanding and the faith to receive whatever God has promised.**

In 2001, after over 12 years on the mission field, the Lord was leading us to return to Texas. We had sold or given away our possessions, and we were going to return to the States in much the same way we had arrived in Chile—with two suitcases per person.

The one thing I had failed to sell was my car. The car had been a blessing for our last few years in Santiago. I had put it up for sale, but there was no interest. As I remember, it was a Thursday morning, and we were due to fly out on Saturday. I was reading my Bible and praying (mostly about the car) when I came to Romans 4:17:

> … *God, who quickeneth the dead, and calleth those things which be not as though they were.*
>
> *Romans 4:17*

When my eyes fell on those words, I heard the Spirit of God say to me, "That's how I do it." My first response was, "Yes, I teach that." Then I realized that I had just heard from God! The Spirit had quickened a truth to my spirit, and I jumped out of my chair and declared, "I call this car sold TODAY, in Jesus' Name!"

Something inside of me was stirred. Faith was born. Words were spoken. The world of the Spirit was in motion!

I had some banking to attend to in town with my assistant pastor, so I drove the car to the appointment. While inside the bank, my cell phone rang. A man was outside, had seen the "for sale" sign in the window of the car, and was interested. I told him to come into the bank, and when I was finished with business, we could talk. A few minutes later I was giving him a ride around the block in my car. He asked what the price was, and when I told him, he immediately said, "I'll take it." I asked how we could make the deal, and he said that his bank was across the street. We made a transfer of funds, visited a notary half a block away and the deal was done. Literally two hours from hearing from God, I was taking my personal belongings out of the car and handing the new owner the keys!

What if I had decided to not spend time with God that morning? What if I had spent my time worrying and plotting how I could leave my car behind and have someone sell it for me? Hearing God made for a very exciting day!

The great need in the church is for individual believers to have their own relationship with God. Many do not know what is meant by the term "hearing God." We often don't know what to expect or how to go about hearing something from the Lord.

We tend to live our lives on the level of the soul. The mind, emotions and the sensations of our circumstances can dominate us to such an extent that we can become hardened to the voice of the Spirit. If we are not sensitive to the things of the Spirit, we look to man for our answers far more than we look to God.

*And the cares of this world, the deceitfulness of riches, and the desires for other things entering in choke the word, and it becomes unfruitful.*

*Mark 4:19*

In his letters, Paul prayed for the believers. His prayers reveal how we can expect God to speak to us. This does not mean that we will hear an audible voice, but there will be a spiritual witness or quickening that will occur as we spend time in His Word. The most important and effective way to hear God is through His Word. Knowing His Word, its context, history and its message to believers will be the foundation for revelation knowledge and hearing Him accurately.

**It will be a "light bulb" moment.**

*Thy word is a lamp unto my feet, and a light unto my path.*

*Psalm 119:105*

How do we hear or what will we hear? If we know what to look for, we will enjoy our time with the Lord and be expectant. If we have no idea what we are looking for or expecting, it can be a very frustrating relationship.

Consider the following prayer of Paul for the Ephesians that we reviewed earlier:

*That the God…may give unto you the spirit of wisdom and revelation in the knowledge of him: The eyes of your understanding being enlightened….*

*Ephesians 1:17–18*

When the Spirit speaks or illumines us, it will be in the area of revelation, wisdom and enlightened understanding. New understanding will come. You will "see" things with spiritual eyes. Confusion will leave, and creativity will take its place. It will be a "light bulb" moment.

> *So then faith cometh by hearing, and hearing by the word of God.*
>
> *Romans 10:17*

Faith will be born when we hear God! A vibrant faith is one of the most important ways to know you have heard God. Faith cannot be fabricated apart from the Word being quickened to our spirits. The hearing we are talking about is spiritual in nature. When the Spirit of God in us is able to break through our minds and emotions and be "quickened" to our spirit, it is called spiritual hearing. Many people "hear" God's Word with their ears, and some hear with their minds alone, but it is our spirits that must hear Him. When His Spirit communicates with our spirit, faith is born.

> *For this cause we also, since the day we heard it, do not cease to pray for you, and to desire that ye might be filled with the knowledge of his will in all wisdom and spiritual understanding; That ye might walk worthy of the Lord unto all pleasing, being fruitful in every good work, and increasing in the knowledge of God.*
>
> *Colossians 1:9–10*

When God speaks there will be vision, direction and energy. He will produce in us all that is within

Him! There will be knowledge of His will and spiritual understanding. We may not have the full picture or know the end from the beginning, but we will know enough to take the next step in faith.

Hearing from God is the key to following Him, and following Him is the key to fulfilling your purpose and destiny. Anything less is hollow and without true value. When we understand that hearing Him is as important to us as it was to Jesus while He was on the earth, we will begin to tune our spiritual eyes and ears to the things of the Spirit.

Chapter Nine

# A REVELATION OF THE FUTURE

Almost everyone wants to know the future. How many mistakes could be avoided if we had some idea what was to come? Is it possible to have a glimpse of the future?

> *However, when He, the Spirit of truth, has come, He will guide you into all truth… and **He will tell you things to come**.*
>
> *John 16:13 NKJV (emphasis mine)*

This really shouldn't surprise us. Faith is the evidence of things not seen. The very nature of faith is to see the unseen and possess it before it manifests. The Spirit of God is in the business of revealing future events, and that revelation births faith in the heart.

Noah was made aware of future events though he

didn't understand them. Yet, the communication from God became his deliverance from the destruction that covered the planet.

> *By faith Noah, being warned of God of things not seen as yet…*
>
> *Hebrews 11:7*

God told Abraham of his destiny and called him to leave his home country without understanding the details. But he knew God was blessing him, giving him an inheritance, and that all the families of the earth would be blessed through him!

> *By faith Abraham, when he was called to go out into a place which he should after receive for an inheritance, obeyed; and he went out, not knowing whither he went.*
>
> *Hebrews 11:8*

Hearing God birthed faith in Moses' heart. He left Egypt because he saw the invisible God, and knew he had a destiny.

> *By faith he (Moses) forsook Egypt, not fearing the wrath of the king: for he endured, as seeing him who is invisible.*
>
> *Hebrews 11:27 (parentheses added)*

Though the future may or not be spelled out in detail, it is the realization that God has spoken that gives birth to faith.

While missionaries in Concepción, Chile, we were extended an invitation to move to the capital city of

Santiago in order to work with a new home group. I had no desire to move to Santiago, which at the time was a city of 5 million people. But as I prayed about the invitation, the Spirit of God spoke to me and showed me three things that were going to happen *when* we moved to Santiago. As soon as I heard the voice of God (the quickening of the Spirit to my spirit), faith was born.

Faith comes by hearing (Romans 10:17). That is the true test to know whether or not you've heard from God. When something is quickened to your spirit, faith is born. There is an excitement and energy that springs forth that wasn't there before. When God showed me three specific things that were going to happen in Santiago, faith filled my heart. All of my natural hesitation disappeared and divine energy consumed me. Within a couple of months we had moved to Santiago, and within a couple of weeks the first thing God had shown me happened. Within a few more weeks the second thing happened and within a few months, the third thing happened. I cannot go into the details in this book, but the three events concerned the home group, the leadership and the new direction that God was going to take the group. The Spirit had revealed to me detailed information, which transformed my heart from one of hesitation to one of faith and peace. He will show you things to come!

In 2007, something similar happened. After living and ministering in Dallas for 6 years, my wife and I took a trip to Colorado to visit Andrew Wommack Ministries and Charis Bible College. We had become acquainted with Andrew's ministry during our years in Dallas, and our grown sons were planning to attend the Bible college. While Betty Kay and I toured the facility, the Spirit of

God spoke to my heart and said, "One day, you will teach here."

I was surprised and perplexed. No one in Colorado knew me. I was currently ministering in Dallas in a small Spanish Bible college at night and on Saturdays and working in a secular job during the day. I had no clue how I would ever teach at Charis. I also didn't understand if what the Spirit had spoken referred to a one-time guest teaching opportunity or a more involved role in the school. But a future event had been revealed to me, and faith was born.

We asked for job applications from AWMI and returned to Dallas. After mailing in our applications, a couple of weeks passed while we prayed about our future. About two weeks later, Betty Kay received a call from the ministry expressing interest in her for an accounting job that was opening. She would need to have an in-person interview and pass some tests, which meant a return trip to Colorado.

*But I had a word from God!* Even though AWMI hadn't called me, there was a possibility for Betty Kay. With a word from God for me and a possible job for Betty Kay, we made the decision to move to Colorado! Where did the faith come from for such a move? It made no sense in the natural. We were in our mid-fifties and launching out once again into a new thing. *But I had a word from God.*

When the Spirit bears witness with your spirit, faith is born, vision is created, energy is released and provision is received.

We moved to Colorado, and Betty Kay got the job. Two weeks passed before I was contacted by the Phone Center of AWMI and offered a job praying for people over the phone. Three months later, I was asked to answer all letters and emails with doctrinal and theological questions that came to the ministry. A year and a half after going to work for AWMI, I was asked to be an impromptu guest speaker for a chapel session of the Bible college. The word from God was fulfilled! But that wasn't all. I was asked to teach approximately ten more times that year. The following year, I was asked to develop and teach nine courses while continuing to answer emails! The year after that, I was hired full time by Charis Bible College and began teaching twelve courses. One year later, I was asked to be the Dean of Students, and more courses were added. When God first spoke to my spirit in early 2007, I never dreamed that things would unfold as they have. I now teach 16 courses and find myself in the most productive time of my life! All of this was born from the Spirit bearing witness with my spirit that "one day" I would teach at Charis Bible College.

The Spirit is longing to show us things to come. Revelation from God is the key to direction, authority, faith, healing, warnings and safety. How many times do we miss the quickening of the Spirit because we are focused on other things? As we read the book of Acts, we can find many examples of the Spirit's involvement in the lives of believers.

> *Then the Spirit said unto Philip, Go near, and join thyself to this chariot.*
>
> *Acts 8:29*

Philip's sensitivity to the Spirit of God brought a high official of the Ethiopian government into saving faith in Jesus. We may not know in this life the impact this one event had on the nation of Ethiopia.

> *While Peter thought on the vision, the Spirit said unto him, Behold, three men seek thee.*
>
> *Acts 10:19*

See how specific the Spirit can be? He doesn't say "some" men, but "three" men. Could you use information like that? Can you expect God to reveal such things to you? You should.

> *And the Spirit bade me go with them, nothing doubting.*
>
> *Acts 11:12*

Concerning this same event, we see that the Spirit wasn't done communicating with Peter. Knowing there were three men wasn't enough. It was also revealed to him that he could confidently go with these men. What if Peter had skipped his prayer time that day and was more concerned with washing his clothes?

**Did you know that the Spirit can reveal worldwide future events as well?**

Did you know that the Spirit can reveal worldwide future events as well? Agabus, a New Testament prophet, was made aware of a coming famine.

*And there stood up one of them named Agabus, and signified by the Spirit that there should be great dearth throughout all the world: which came to pass in the days of Claudius Caesar.*

*Acts 11:28*

Consider this passage about Paul and Barnabas being sent out as apostolic missionaries.

*As they ministered to the Lord, and fasted, the Holy Ghost said, Separate me Barnabas and Saul for the work whereunto I have called them.*

*Acts 13:2*

It is interesting that the Spirit didn't reveal the nature of the work unto which He had called Barnabas and Saul (Paul). That is because they already knew. The Spirit had revealed their purpose months or even years before, but Barnabas and Paul were waiting on God's timing. As I learned after our first missionary trip to Mexico in 1978, the call is not the sending. More on that later.

*After they had come to Mysia, they tried to go into Bithynia, but the Spirit did not permit them.*

*Acts 16:7 NKJV*

Here we see the Spirit redirecting the apostles. Because they were in motion and following the first words of the Spirit, they were in a place to receive more. We seldom get the whole story the first time when hearing God. But as we walk in what we know, more will come. The key is to remain sensitive to the Holy Spirit.

As you can see, the Spirit can be very active in our

lives. These examples include instructions, direction, information, revelation of the future and re-direction.

All believers have access to the ministry of the Holy Spirit. Are we listening and expecting to hear Him?

> *He that hath an ear, let him hear what the Spirit saith.*
>
> *Revelation 2:7*

We tend to live our lives with our sight focused on the present and perhaps a few days ahead. If we think about the future at all, it is usually to hope that everything works out well or hope nothing bad will happen to us.

If we become afflicted with a sickness or some other challenge comes our way, we become very focused on the present, and the future is seen with dread. Will we make it past this storm of life? Can we have the future revealed to us by the Spirit?

There are two verses in the book of Hebrews that have given me a key to overcoming obstacles and having peace in the midst of the challenges of life.

> *By faith he forsook Egypt, not fearing the wrath of the king: for* ***he endured, as seeing him who is invisible.***
>
> *Hebrews 11:27 (emphasis mine)*

Moses endured by seeing Him who is invisible! We have two sets of eyes or two kinds of vision. Our natural eyes see only what is visible, but our spiritual eyes can see into the world of the Spirit. Seeing the invisible is the key to overcoming the visible! Here is the second verse that has helped me.

> *Now faith is the substance of things hoped for,* ***the evidence of things not seen.***
>
> *Hebrews 11:1 (emphasis mine)*

As we have seen, faith comes by hearing God's Word in our spirit. Faith takes us immediately into the realm of things not seen. We don't need faith for what can we see, but for what we can't see with our natural eyes. When we see the future with our spiritual eyes, we know that faith has come, and it will carry us through to victory. Spiritual vision is simply another way of speaking of revelation knowledge. The Spirit bears witness with our spirit concerning present circumstances and future events.

> **I am going to pass through the storm successfully.**

Whenever I have been challenged physically or am facing some other obstacle in my life, I have learned to switch over to my spiritual eyes. I look into the future, and if I can see myself healed, whole, prosperous, playing with my grandkids and enjoying life with my wife, I know I am going to pass through the storm successfully. Rather than focusing on the temporal challenge and becoming fearful and full of doubt, I endure by seeing the unseen.

As long as I can look into the future and "see" myself fulfilling my purpose in God, I know any current challenge is temporal. It will pass. I will overcome.

Too often believers become consumed with the temporal, with the doctor's report, with politics and with financial challenges. They don't stop to look into the future or to see Him who is unseen. They try to win their battles with their own strength and limited vision—and often fail. The key to the abundant life is revelation knowledge.

**Such revelation will usually only come from communion with God in the Word and in the Spirit.**

> *This is my comfort in my affliction: for thy word hath quickened me.*
>
> *Psalm 119:50*

Chapter Ten

# THE REVELATION OF WORDS

I was sitting in my recliner flipping through channels on the TV when I came to the beginning of a movie I thought might be interesting. I can't remember what the movie was now because I never saw it. As the graphics for the opening credits were rolling, I "saw" something else that captured my attention.

The graphics filled the screen with the letters of the alphabet floating in nothingness. Then out of the thousands of letters, certain letters began to arrange themselves and form words. The words were obviously describing the title of the movie, the producer, director, actors, etc., but I was seeing something else. I instantly saw the world of the Spirit and how creative words were available to us constantly. His Word is alive and active, and suddenly I realized that all of God's words are alive and "floating" in the world of the Spirit, waiting to be spoken and **to be given an assignment!**

From the opening credits of a movie, the Spirit of God had quickened me to see into another dimension and comprehend the power of words. I turned off the TV and began to meditate on what the Lord had shown me. Scriptures began to flood my heart and mind.

Let's begin by considering God's words.

> *So shall My word be that goes forth from My mouth; It shall not return to Me void, But it shall accomplish what I please, And it shall prosper in the thing for which I sent it.*
>
> *Isaiah 55:11 NKJV*

God's words accomplish God's purposes. In the beginning was the Word, and the Word was with God and was God. God created all things by speaking. He called those things which were not as though they were. The things that we see were made from that which does not appear. Just as I saw in the opening of the movie, the vast potential for creative words existed in the space of infinity but only took shape once they were assigned. God has created all things out of His very nature (He is the Word) and has given tangible form to creation by speaking! He called that which was not, and it became what He assigned it to be. The Bible then declares that He upholds all things by the word of His power (Hebrews 1:3).

Every word God has spoken has an eternal assignment and will continually accomplish its purpose. God's Word cannot fail. It lives and abides forever.

How does that impact our lives? As I thought on these things, more scriptures filled my heart. We were created in the image of God. We have the capacity to speak His words. In fact, we were created to hear His words, live by them and repeat them. Not only *may* we repeat them, the use of God's words in our mouths is how God has designed creation to be governed! We are "word creations," meaning we were created by the Word, we exist by the Word, we must live by hearing the Word and we are free to speak the Word to accomplish God's purposes in our lives and in the world!

**Every word God has spoken has an eternal assignment and will continually accomplish its purpose.**

How did Jesus describe this?

> *... for out of the abundance of the heart the mouth speaketh. A good man out of the good treasure of the heart bringeth forth good things...*
>
> *Matthew 12:34-35*

This is amazing but true. Just as God brought forth what was in His heart (the universe, earth, you and me), Jesus declares that out of our hearts we can "bring forth" good things! How? Out of the abundance of the heart,the mouth speaks! It is our speaking from what is in our hearts that can "bring forth" good things in our lives. Out of the spiritual dimension of God's nature, purpose and love, we find His words. We are called to live by those words, let them fill our hearts, and then bring them into being by speaking. Could this be true?

> *For verily I say unto you, That whosoever shall say unto this mountain, Be thou removed, and be thou cast into the sea; and shall not doubt in his heart, but shall believe that those things which he saith shall come to pass;* ***he shall have whatsoever he saith.***
>
> *Mark 11:23 (emphasis mine)*

Do you believe that you can have what you say? Well, if the abundance of your heart is filled with the abundance of God's heart, then yes, you may! Out of the abundance of your heart you may speak, declare, and assign God's words to the mountains of your life, and those words will accomplish His purpose!

When His Word is in our hearts, words that have been quickened to our spirits (and faith comes by hearing His words), then the spirit of faith will speak.

> *We having the same spirit of faith, according as it is written, I believed, and therefore have I spoken; we also believe, and therefore speak.*
>
> *2 Corinthians 4:13*

Can the mountains in our lives be removed? If you are bringing forth from the abundance of your heart the good things of His Word which have been revealed to you, then yes, you can assign those words to your mountain, and it will move. It has no choice.

> *Is not my word like as a fire? saith the Lord; and like a hammer that breaketh the rock in pieces?*
>
> *Jeremiah 23:29*

Think of this in the realm of healing. God's will is health and healing. God's nature is health and healing. Jesus healed all who were oppressed with sickness because He came to do God's will.

> *He sent his word, and healed them, and delivered them from their destructions.*
>
> *Psalm 107:20*

He sent His word. He sent His Word. He sent His WORD and healed us. His Word declares that by His stripes you *were* healed! (1 Peter 2:24) The same verse that was quickened to me so many years ago in Guatemala is the Word which is alive and active and has been assigned to heal YOU! If you will let it fill your heart, from your heart you can bring forth your healing by speaking!

As I continued to meditate on the words I saw on the TV screen, the revelation continued to deepen. God's words are alive, eternal and available to be spoken by those who have heard them. If those words are in your heart, then all that remains is to give them an assignment by speaking.

> *A man's belly shall be satisfied with the fruit of his mouth; and with the increase of his lips shall he be filled.*
>
> *Proverbs 18:20*

Could it be that we can be satisfied and see increase in our lives by simply speaking? I began to practice what I was learning by speaking words—words that had been quickened to me by the Spirit. Words of life, health, prosperity, blessing, favor and purpose began to come from my heart and out of my mouth. I wasn't even speaking whole sentences at times—just words. I began speaking them over myself, my family and my God-given purpose. And what is happening? Doors of opportunity are opening, blessings are overtaking me, and my family is experiencing favor and increase.

I began to see myself differently. God Almighty lives within me, and His words are alive and active in me, fully charged, awaiting an assignment. It's how God created the universe, and it is how God wants you to take charge of your life.

> *For all the promises of God in him are yea, and in him Amen, unto the glory of God by us.*
>
> *2 Corinthians 1:20*

His promises are words. They are life-giving, healing, delivering, protecting, uplifting, prospering words of blessing and grace. They are all yes and amen to the glory of God *by us!* We are the ones who must believe with our hearts and confess with our mouths. All that has been quickened to our spirits can be spoken, and with the increase of our lips we shall be filled!

Though many of these truths were already real to me, I entered into a new dimension of revelation by watching the opening credits of a Hollywood movie. The Spirit of God was using my surroundings to speak to me. This happens all of the time because I am always looking for more revelation. I am sensitive to it. No doubt, thousands of Christians have seen that same three minutes of that movie and nothing happened. But if your heart is devoted to hearing God, you will find revelation in the most interesting places and circumstances of life. God is always speaking!

## Chapter Eleven

# HE WILL GUIDE YOU INTO ALL TRUTH

I have often been struck by the dullness of hearing in many Christians. As I have ministered and heard others minister, I have had the opportunity to spend time with those who were listening to the messages. I have often wondered if they were in the same room hearing the same message that I heard. For example, a response to a message of healing has often been diametrically opposed to the truth that was just presented. Rather than being stirred in faith and excited about receiving from God, some remain fixated on explaining why they are sick or give great detail to everything that is wrong with them and everything the doctor has said. It is as if there is a cloud of dullness over their hearts and minds.

> *Of whom we have many things to say, and hard to be uttered, seeing ye are* ***dull of hearing.***
>
> *Hebrews 5:11 (emphasis mine)*

As I meditated on this, I wondered how often it had been true of me as well. How many truths had I heard but not heard in years past? How long had it taken for the Word to penetrate my dull mind and heart? How much more truth is the Holy Spirit trying to get through to me even now?

How can we come to a place of "hearing" with our hearts? It is the Truth that makes us free, but so many are walking in bondage, ignorance, brokenness and fear. They obviously aren't "hearing" the gospel.

> *Draw near to God, and he will draw near to you. Cleanse your hands, you sinners, and purify your hearts, you double-minded.*
>
> *James 4:8 NKJV*

Dullness of hearing is a heart issue. It is a sin issue. Sin distracts us, hardens our hearts and dulls our hearing. As much as we don't want to hear that (no pun intended), it is true. If we draw near to God with sincere hearts, He WILL draw near to us. If there is a cloud of dullness in our lives, it is due to an impure heart. It may not be a heart filled with evil, but simply a heart filled with the cares of the world. We all deal with that. But double mindedness is a huge barrier to hearing God. Remember those who sought Jesus for healing? They were focused.

> *You will seek me and find me, when you seek me with all your heart.*
>
> *Jeremiah 29:13*

This isn't a test or an obstacle course that God has put in front of us. It is simply a reality. For a heart to receive from God, it must be open to hearing God. Obviously, anything that is distracting the heart will be a barrier to hearing God.

How will the Spirit speak to us? The Spirit of God will always confirm and reveal the Word of God. Truth is not defined by human emotion and feeling. That is why the heart must be focused on Him rather than on circumstances and emotions. Truth is not relative to our culture or what is currently politically correct. Truth is not based on what the doctor says or the politician or lawyer. Truth is spiritual. The Holy Spirit is called the Spirit of truth.

> *Howbeit when he, the Spirit of truth, is come, he will guide you into all truth.*
>
> *John 16:13*

Jesus is the Way, the Truth and the Life. He is full of grace and truth. If we abide in His Word, we shall know the truth, and the truth shall make us free. It is the Spirit of Truth that lives within for the express purpose of knowing Him—the Truth. Why then are there so many different doctrines, interpretations and opinions about truth?

Part of Paul's prayer in Ephesians 1 makes clear what the need really is.

*The eyes of your understanding being enlightened; that ye may know what is the hope of his calling, and what (are) the riches of the glory of his inheritance in the saints.*

*Ephesians 1:18 (parentheses added)*

Paul prayed that the eyes of our understanding would be enlightened so we might know: 1) His calling in our lives and 2) our inestimable value to Him! This knowledge can only come from the Holy Spirit. It is revelation knowledge. It is this truth that will set you free, reveal your true identity, unlock the promises of God and establish you in your unique purpose in life.

This revelation will usually be progressive and unfold as we grow in the Lord. The glories of the kingdom are available to all who will seek, ask and knock. Creating the right environment to hear Him is the secret. These mysteries are now available to be revealed.

*But as it is written, Eye hath not seen, nor ear heard, neither have entered into the heart of man, the things which God hath prepared for them that love him.* ***But God hath revealed them unto us by his Spirit:*** *for the Spirit searcheth all things, yea, the deep things of God.*

*1 Corinthians 2:9–10 (emphasis mine)*

Your true identity, purpose and inheritance are waiting to be unlocked and discovered. They exist in your re-born spirit, but it is His Spirit that does the unlocking. The Spirit searches out the deep things of God and reveals them to us. Many times our understanding is limited. Some revelations may take years for us to fully comprehend. Others are immediately understood. As we walk in the light that we have, more light comes.

> *Now to Him who is able to establish you according to my gospel and the preaching of Jesus Christ, according to* ***the revelation of the mystery*** *kept secret since the world began* ***but now made manifest, and by the prophetic Scriptures*** *made known to all nations.*
>
> *Romans 16:25-26 NKJV (emphasis mine)*

The Spirit is not going to contradict the Word of God.

Revelation knowledge is made known by the Scriptures! As David said, "Thy word is a lamp unto my feet, and a light unto my path." (Psalm 119:105)

> *The entrance of thy words giveth light; it giveth understanding unto the simple.*
>
> *Psalm 119:130*

His Word is a light that shines in a dark place. His Word gives light and understanding to the simple and is a light unto our path.

**Revelation knowledge is the quickening work of the Spirit by the Word to the heart of man so that we might know all that God has prepared for us!**

When we speak of revelation knowledge or the Spirit bearing witness with our spirit (Romans 8:16), we are speaking of the Spirit of God revealing the realities of our recreated spirit. It must be understood that the Spirit of God is going to remain true to the Word of God. The

Spirit and the Word agree. In fact, the sword of the Spirit is the Word!

> *And take the helmet of salvation, and the sword of* ***the Spirit, which is the word of God.***
>
> *Ephesians 6:17 (emphasis mine)*

The Spirit is not going to contradict the Word of God. When we speak of revelation knowledge, we are not speaking of some "new" revelation that is not biblical. Revelation knowledge unlocks the Truth of the Word to your spirit, which opens your eyes and gives birth to faith and vision.

Jesus said that His words were Spirit and life.

> *The words that I speak unto you, they are spirit, and they are life.*
>
> *John 6:63*

The Spirit confirms the Word. The Spirit and the Word are not separate. Consider the role of the Word in the life of a believer, and you will understand the role of the Spirit. The Spirit gives words of wisdom and knowledge (1 Corinthians 12:8). *All scripture is given by inspiration of God, and is profitable for doctrine, for reproof, for correction, for instruction in righteousness* (2 Timothy 3:16). Thus, the Spirit also reproves, corrects and instructs.

Guilt and condemnation don't come from God. But wisdom, knowledge, correction and instruction will be quickened to your spirit. Let the Spirit minister to you by the Word. Even a word of reproof is truth, and the truth will make you free! (John 8:31-32)

The truth of healing will make you free from sickness. The truth of His provision will make you free from lack. The truth of His protection will make you free from fear. The truth of His love will make you free from torment. The truth of His grace will make you free from guilt and condemnation. The truth of His victory will make you free from weakness. As His truth is quickened to us by the Spirit and the Word, we will know the hope of His calling and be equipped to walk in the victory He has prepared for us.

> *If ye continue in my word, then are ye my disciples indeed; And ye shall know the truth, and the truth shall make you free.*
>
> *John 8:31–32*

Chapter Twelve

# THE STIRRING OF YOUR SPIRIT

The more we are continually filled with the Spirit, the more prepared we will be for the storms of life that come our way. There have been a number of times in my life when I can't say I heard a word from God, but my spirit was stirred within as I heard the word of man! Faith was born at hearing a negative report. Was faith born from the *negative* report? No. The negative report caused my spirit to be stirred within me and respond with God's Word!

> *Now while Paul waited for them at Athens,* ***His spirit was stirred in him....***
>
> *Acts 17:16 (emphasis mine)*

Paul saw the idolatry of Athens, and that darkness stirred his spirit. Many times our futures are changed because our spirits get stirred.

In 1978, during our short 4 months in Mexico, my wife had serious complications from pregnancy. We submitted to the normal exams and a sonogram in order to understand what was going on. The next day, I went by myself to get the results of the tests. I didn't expect the doctor's verdict, however. "The fetus has died. The sac has collapsed. There will be a spontaneous abortion."

I didn't go to hear the doctor's report that day with a firm word from God. I wasn't sure what was going on, and I certainly had no idea he would say what he did. But when I heard those words, "The fetus is dead," my spirit was stirred within me. Something deep down inside responded with an authoritative "NO!" Was that me or was it the Spirit of God? It was the Spirit of God within me! In much the same way that Jesus responded to the news of the death of the daughter of Jairus, the Spirit responded within me.

> *While he yet spake, there came from the ruler of the synagogue's house certain which said, Thy daughter is dead: why troublest thou the Master any further?* ***As soon as Jesus heard the word that was spoken, he saith unto the ruler of the synagogue, Be not afraid, only believe.***
>
> *Mark 5:35-36 (emphasis mine)*

Rather than let fear express itself in words, let the Word crush the fear! The revelation of our identity, authority and God's purpose for our lives is all the ammunition you need when you hear a negative report.

I chose to not repeat the doctor's report to my wife. I told her to rest in bed and that all would be well. We continued to stand in faith. My spirit was stirred to resist the negative diagnosis and to receive a miracle. We didn't return to that doctor. Several months later, my son David was born—completely healthy and full of life!

Twice when I have heard the word of the doctor concerning my own health, my spirit was stirred within me. Twice I have known that their words were not the last word. Twice I have opted to not follow their wishes, and both times I was healed within two days.

I am not speaking against doctors or medicine. In other situations, I have followed the doctor's instructions. I had faith and peace to do so. But there are times when your spirit gets stirred, and the knowledge of your inheritance in Christ causes a spiritual reaction that transcends the natural circumstances. This is a characteristic of revelation knowledge. The Spirit bore witness with my spirit that God had made provision for me.

**Rather than let fear express itself in words, let the Word crush the fear!**

The only way that one can respond in faith to a negative report is by having already established a strong foundation in the Word. It is in knowing God's Word, His promises and His nature that it becomes possible to instantly recognize the voice of fear and destruction. He is for you and not against you!

> *And a stranger will they not follow, but will flee from him: for they know not the voice of strangers.*
>
> *John 10:5*

To the degree that you know the voice of God and have a revelation of His Truth, you will also recognize the voice of a stranger. The "stranger" will attempt to sow fear, destroy faith and bring your focus off of God and onto your own strength and resources. But if you know the voice of God, the voice of the stranger will stir your spirit to lay hold of God's promises. Faith can come alive as a reaction to the negative report.

Probably the biggest hindrance to God's people hearing Him can be found in our un-renewed minds. If we aren't thinking His thoughts, how easy will it be to hear His voice? How sensitive will we be to a negative report? Will our spirits be stirred or will they passively receive bad news? If our minds are filled with all of the trivia, the news, the fears and stresses of the world, are we in a good place to "hear" God or "see" His will for our lives? Probably not.

Many believers have no dominion over their thought lives. They are the ones who usually have trouble hearing from God or having a clear direction for their lives. What we think about can be a barrier or an open door to the voice of God. What does a renewed mind mean for us?

> *And be not conformed to this world: but be ye transformed by the renewing of your mind,* ***that ye may prove what is that good, and acceptable, and perfect, will of God.***
>
> *Romans 12:2 (emphasis mine)*

The renewing of our minds transforms us. It gives us the ability to prove (to know) the perfect will of God. In other words, an un-renewed mind, one full of negative thoughts, doubts, fears and stress, can't tap into the good, acceptable and perfect will of God. The voice of God is going to be filtered through what is in our minds. Sometimes our minds are so full of junk that we can't hear God at all. Other times, we may hear Him but misunderstand or misinterpret His leading due to all of the filters we have allowed to remain—filters of negativity, doubt, self-centeredness, etc.

It can be compared to listening to your favorite music in the middle of a busy, downtown street versus listening in the quiet of your living room. You will miss a lot in the downtown setting. The distractions and noise will block your reception of the music that is being played. So it is with our thought life. Purging our minds of "junk" thoughts is crucial to being ready to hear Him and discover His perfect will for our lives.

This is important when you receive a negative report. If your mind is filled with the negative things of the world, the negative report will likely find a home in your heart. But if your heart and mind are filled with the promises of God and a revelation of your inheritance in Christ, a negative report will stir your spirit to resist the enemy and receive God's provision and victory.

*He wakeneth mine ear to hear....*

*Isaiah 50:4*

Peg - Jer 15:16-21

Chapter Thirteen

# THE SECRET PLACE

We must create an environment to hear God. We make time for what is important to us. I believe hearing from God should be the most important thing in our lives. *"Man shall not live by bread alone, but by every word that proceedeth out of the mouth of God."* (Matthew 4:4) Any living we do apart from God's Word isn't true living. It can't be. Men were created to live by hearing God. He alone is the Source of life, light and purpose.

What we feed on is the fuel of our lives. Our bodies feed on food. Our minds feed on information. Our souls feed on events, relationships and emotions. And our spirits must feed on the Word, which is Spirit.

> *Your words were found, and I ate them, And Your word was to me the joy and rejoicing of my heart.*
>
> *Jeremiah 15:16 NKJV*

Which "food" is more important to you? The answer will reveal a lot about your present and your future. Those who focus on natural food will talk about food, think about food, crave food and live their lives around food. Those who feed on information will fill their minds with all of the latest news on whatever subject interests them. They struggle when separated from the latest information. It is what satisfies them. Those who feed the soul are subject to emotional ups and downs. They crave acceptance and applause. When they don't receive the affirmation of others, they flounder.

While all of these areas comprise the reality of our lives, they should not be the source of our lives. We are spiritual beings created to live by and feed on the Word of God. Jesus said, "Man shall not live on bread alone but by every word that proceeds from the mouth of God." In other words, though we must eat and relate to our world and those around us, those areas cannot be the source of our lives. Only His words can satisfy and give us the strength and wisdom to live above the corruption in the world.

So…what are you feeding on? If your focus and passion isn't God's Word, you will never be satisfied. The other areas I've mentioned will begin to dominate your life and leave you unfulfilled and stressed. A spirit that is nourished on God's words will produce life and peace. This happens in the "secret place."

> *He that dwelleth in* ***the secret place*** *of the most High shall abide under the shadow of the Almighty.*
>
> *Psalm 91:1(emphasis mine)*

How do we create this "secret place?" What does it look like? The truth is, it isn't really a place but rather an attitude. That does not mean that we can't have a special place of study and prayer, but the true secret place with God is in our hearts.

As I have mentioned, hearing God has a lot to do with having His Word alive in our hearts. The hardened or distracted heart will always be slow to hear or insensitive to the quickening of the Spirit.

> *Abide in Me, and I in you. As the branch cannot bear fruit of itself, unless it abides in the vine, neither can you, unless you abide in Me. I am the vine, you are the branches. He who abides in Me, and I in him, bears much fruit; for without Me you can do nothing.*
>
> *John 15:4–5 NKJV*

Abiding in Him is spiritual food. The branch needs continual nourishment from the vine or it will dry up. Just as the body needs physical food, our spirits need the food of God's Word, which is Spirit. We were created to draw our lives from communion with the Father. If we renew our minds to the knowledge of God and neglect to spend time with Him in communion, our faith will be mental and not truly spiritual.

> *As newborn babes, desire the sincere milk of the word that you may grow thereby.*
>
> *1 Peter 2:2*

The Word nourishes our spirit man. Our re-born spirit is complete and lacks nothing, but that does not mean we can live a life that is separated from the Source.

*And I, brethren, could not speak unto you as unto spiritual, but as unto carnal, even as unto babes in Christ.*

*1 Corinthians 3:1*

Paul did not consider all Christians as "spiritual." Though they were born again, they hadn't grown in the Word. Therefore, they were either carnal (sense ruled) or they were babes who had yet to grow.

*That we should no longer be children...but, speaking the truth in love, may grow up in all things into Him who is the head—Christ.*

*Ephesians 4:14–15 NKJV*

Paul was very aware of the need for believers to be sustained by their relationship with the Father. His prayers and exhortations continually pointed to this communion. Continual communion with the Father through the Word is the foundation for hearing God.

Jesus prayed, *"I have given them thy word".* (John 17:14) Hearing from God has much to do with recognizing the inestimable gift of the Word of God. The Word is His Truth. His Word sanctifies us (sets us apart for His purpose). His words are Spirit. Hearing Him should be normal.

*Now we have received, not the spirit of the world, but the spirit which is of God; that we might know the things that are freely given to us of God.*

*1 Corinthians 2:12 NKJV*

The things God has given us, our inheritance in Him

(which includes healing, authority, joy, peace, provision, protection, deliverance, vision and purpose) is revealed to us by the Spirit and the Word. As we keep our eyes, ears and hearts focused on Him, the Spirit will bear witness with our spirit of these new creation realities, faith will be born and victories won!

> *I will meditate also of all thy work, and talk of thy doings.*
>
> *Psalm 77:12*

What does it mean to meditate in God's Word? We have all heard the expression, "You are what you eat," but it is also true to say, "You are what you think."

> *For as he thinks in his heart, so is he.*
>
> *Proverbs 23:7*

You are what you are today because of the things that you have allowed your heart to dwell on. What you focus on today is building your tomorrow. Hearing God is a fruit of having a heart sensitive to His Word. Having a sensitive heart comes from biblical meditation. Biblical meditation should not be confused with the mindless chanting of Eastern religions. Here are some definitions to consider:

**Whether we realize it or not, we all spend a great deal of our time each day in meditation.**

Meditate: to engage in contemplation or

reflection, to focus one's thoughts on, reflect or ponder over, to plan or project in the mind.

Think: to form or have in the mind, to have as an opinion, to regard as or consider, to reflect on or ponder, to determine by reflecting, to call to mind or remember, to center one's thoughts on or form a mental picture of, to have in the mind engaged in reflection, to consider.

Reflect: to think quietly and calmly

Ponder: to weigh in the mind, to think about, reflect on, to think about—especially quietly, soberly and deeply.

Whether we realize it or not, we all spend a great deal of our time each day in meditation. Far too often, we meditate on, think about and ponder circumstances, perceived lack, frustrations, worries and the negative words of others. If we would spend more time meditating on the nature of the Father, the blessings of the covenant, the promises of God and His Word, it would be life and peace to us!

It is meditation in God's Word, His promises and His nature that creates the environment in which things will be quickened to our spirits. True hearing will take place. There will be confirmation, direction, comfort and vision imparted. Not only will our minds be renewed, our hearts will be attentive to the Spirit.

Jesus said, *"For where your treasure is, there will your heart be also."* (Matthew 6:21) Only when our treasure is hearing Him will our hearts be in the "secret place." Like Jeremiah, we will say, *"Thy words were found, and I did eat them; and thy word was unto me the joy and rejoicing of mine heart."* (Jeremiah 15:16)

This is true meditation and will open our spiritual eyes and ears to see and hear all that we have received in Christ.

… *to be spiritually minded is life and peace.*

*Romans 8:6*

Chapter Fourteen

# GOD IS THINKING ABOUT YOU!

Did you know that God thinks about you? Not only that, He thinks thoughts of peace about you, not evil.

> *For I know the thoughts that I think toward you, saith the Lord, thoughts of peace, and not of evil, to give you an expected end.*
>
> *Jeremiah 29:11*

God's thoughts can be understood by witnessing the ministry of Jesus. *"For the Son of man is not come to destroy men's lives, but to save them."* (Luke 9:56) God is thinking about deliverance, salvation, healing, prosperity and the abundant life. That is His nature.

A key to receiving revelation knowledge from God begins with understanding His heart toward you and His thoughts about you. God is not unaware, distant and silent until we cry out. He is continually thinking thoughts of life and peace toward you. His infinite love is continually aimed at you. God's thoughts are focused on your health and wellbeing. He desires to give you an expected end. "End" means "future." God is thinking about your future!

A parent or a grandparent is often focused on how to do good things for their children or grandchildren. They are often planning ahead for the next birthday party, holiday or vacation. Though the child may have no idea of what is being planned, there is an "expected end" that is being considered by the parent or grandparent. As a parent and grandparent myself, I take great delight in finding ways to bless my children and grandchildren. God is much more excited about blessing His children than even the most generous parent!

A concept of a distant, uninterested God will only serve as a barrier to hearing Him.

It may be hard for us to comprehend that God's thoughts and even God's words are constant. We could say that He is always "on" or as Paul declared, His promises are "yes" and "amen." (2 Corinthians 1:20) In other words, God has no off days, no weeks of silence and no moment in which His words and thoughts switch off. His Word is alive and active! (Hebrews 4:12) He is thinking about you as you read this. The verses I am quoting are as alive as when they were spoken by God the first time.

Getting our minds in tune with this reality is

foundational in learning to receive revelation knowledge. A concept of a distant, uninterested God will only serve as a barrier to hearing Him.

God's thoughts about your future aren't seen, but they are just as real as the sun coming up tomorrow. We could say that faith is embracing God's thoughts about your future *right now*. God is thinking about your health, your prosperity, your success, your peace, your joy and your divine purpose. What are YOU thinking about? When your thoughts agree with God's thoughts, you are in a place of hearing from Him. As long as we are double minded about God's thoughts, we won't receive from Him (James 1:6-8).

Just like the electricity in a house is always on and ready for use, God's Word and the Spirit are always on. If we aren't hearing Him, it isn't because He isn't speaking. Just as an old radio has to be tuned to the correct frequency in order for the listener to clearly hear the station, our minds and thoughts must be in tune with the Spirit of God. A key to this is to think God's thoughts.

> *Finally, brethren, whatsoever things are true, whatsoever things are honest, whatsoever things are just, whatsoever things are pure, whatsoever things are lovely, whatsoever things are of good report; if there be any virtue, and if there be any praise,* ***think on these things.***
>
> *Philippians 4:8 (emphasis mine)*

This is how God thinks about you, and it is how you should think. He is thinking things that are true, honest, pure, lovely and worthy of praise about you! Taking your thoughts captive to the true, honest and lovely thoughts of

God will open your heart to receive revelation knowledge and to hear Him.

God's revelations to our hearts will exactly represent His thoughts, which are expressed by His Word. The more we can agree with the thoughts of God and the words of God, the more attuned we will be to the Spirit of God who wishes to make those things alive and real within us. Again, we can call it "hearing" or "seeing" or "revelation knowledge." Whatever we call it, it happens when we come into contact with the Spirit of God, and the things of God are revealed to our hearts.

God is thinking about you, loves you and desires to have you receive from Him.

> *The counsel of the Lord standeth for ever, the thoughts of his heart to all generations.*
>
> *Psalm 33:11*

Chapter Fifteen

# RECEIVING REVELATION

The greatest need in the church today is truth that springs from revelation knowledge. There are far too many well-meaning Christians who will follow certain teachers and swallow anything they say. They don't even realize that they at times are receiving a Genetically Altered Gospel (GAG). Truth is being mixed with untruth. The reliability of God's Word is even challenged, and only parts are believed. The typical Christian who may not be in tune with the Spirit of God might not notice wrong teaching and quickly be led astray.

As Christians, we have a responsibility to understand the whole counsel of God, to know the Word and to be able to correct, instruct and exhort with all patience. The wisdom of God is available to us but can only be spiritually discerned.

*But the natural man receiveth not the things of the Spirit of God: for they are foolishness unto him: neither can he know them, because they are spiritually discerned.*

*1 Corinthians 2:14*

Sadly, there are many "natural" Christians who aren't really hearing God or having His truths revealed to their spirits. The things of the Kingdom are contained in scripture, but they are only revealed from Spirit to spirit—from His to ours. *The Spirit bears witness with our spirit* (Romans 8:16).

Jesus said, *"Unto you it is given to know the mystery of the kingdom of God: but unto them that are without, all these things are done in parables."* Mark 4:11

Paul said, *"But we speak the wisdom of God in a mystery, even the hidden wisdom, which God ordained before the world unto our glory."* 1Corinthians 2:7

In other words, there are things God wants us to know and mysteries He wants to reveal. This is not impossible or even difficult. It is His will. But if we haven't created the environment to hear Him, we will have to live without.

Adam and Eve were created to learn directly from God. The capacity to have close communion with Him was lost through sin. Man became fearful, ignorant and darkened. Today, many go to church or read their Bibles in order to learn *about* God, but only some press in to know Him and learn *from* Him. There is a difference! Fallen men walk in the vanity of their minds, have their understanding darkened and are alienated from the life of God because of ignorance and the blindness of their hearts (Ephesians 4:17-18). The Spirit of God wants to lead us into all truth, but we must be willing to be led.

> *Howbeit when he, the Spirit of truth, is come, he will guide you into all truth.*
>
> *John 16:13*

As long as we have no interest in hearing from God, vanity and ignorance will be our environment *even if we are born again!* Just because the Spirit of God lives within does not mean that the mysteries of God and His promises will automatically be real to us.

Who were you, and who are you?

> *For ye were sometimes darkness, but now are ye light in the Lord: walk as children of light.*
>
> *Ephesians 5:8*

All that Adam lost for himself and for all mankind has been restored through Christ. We not only walked in darkness, we *were* darkness. Spiritual revelation was not possible as it is now. But in Christ we have been plugged back in to the Source, and we are light! In other words, the light of life has entered and transformed our spirits. We are once again in a position to have communion with God. We can hear Him with our spirits.

God wants to reveal things to us—from the smallest details of life to the greatest revelations of Kingdom mysteries. All of these mysteries and truths exist in our recreated spirits, but they must be revealed to us if they are going to be real to us. The question is, will we allow our spirits to be quickened by His Spirit?

There are two keys to becoming sensitive to the Spirit of God and revelation knowledge.

The first is to appreciate, value and esteem God's Word. How we approach God's Word is key to whether or not we will receive revelation from Him.

*My son, attend to my words; incline thine ear unto my sayings.*

*Proverbs 4:20*

We were created in the image of God, and *"in the beginning was the Word and the Word was with God and the Word was God."* (John 1:1) In other words, we were created in the image of the eternal, living Word that created all things and was made flesh. That means that we were created to live by the Word. We can hear the Word, respond to the Word, feed on the Word, speak the Word and do the Word. Hearing Him should become natural to us. We were created to hear Him!

## Hearing Him should come "natural" to us.

As you spend time in His Word, expect the Spirit to quicken truth to you. Expect to be enlightened. Your time in the Word is the door to hearing God.

The second key is to pray in the Spirit. The more time we spend praying in the Spirit (the prayer language of tongues), the more in tune we will be with the Spirit of God.

*For he that speaketh in an unknown tongue speaketh not unto men, but unto God: for no man understandeth him; howbeit in the spirit he speaketh mysteries.*

*1 Corinthians 14:2*

When you pray in the Spirit, you are speaking the mysteries of God. The more time you devote to this, the more your spirit man will become sensitive and alive to those mysteries. You will notice spiritual understanding increasing. Specific words from God will come alive to you. You will begin to see and hear the things of God because you are edifying yourself in your spirit (1 Corinthians 14:4, 14).

*O generation, see ye the word of the Lord....*

*Jeremiah 2:31*

Chapter Sixteen

# ACCORDING TO HIS PURPOSE

Hearing God or receiving revelation knowledge should impact every area of our lives. There is no area more important than the discovery of your unique purpose and calling. Each of us has been created with a purpose and a destiny. The revelation of who we are in Christ should be followed by the revelation of what we are meant to do.

> *...the Holy Ghost said, Separate me Barnabas and Saul for the work whereunto I have called them.*
>
> *Acts 13:2*

The works ordained for us will change and evolve over the years. Nevertheless, the more sensitive we are to the Spirit of God, the more aware we will be to the times and seasons of our lives. As we grow in grace, we will also move from victory to victory—if we are in communion with the Spirit of God.

It is interesting that in Acts 13:2, the Holy Spirit does not mention what work He has called Barnabas and Paul to accomplish. That is because it wasn't a surprise or a new thing they had never considered. I believe they had known for months or years what the work was, but they were waiting for the perfect timing before moving into the call. How many of us have "jumped the gun" in the past, only to find that we had the right call but the wrong timing?

In 1978, my new wife, Betty Kay, and I set out for Mexico in my yellow Volkswagen. All of our belongings were in and on the car, and we had $300 in cash. Our goal was to study Spanish in Guadalajara and move into a missionary ministry somewhere in the nation. I thought I had heard from God. We had visited Mexico the summer before with a team from our Bible College, and the call of God had been awakened in my heart. However, at that time, I didn't know the difference between the calling and the sending.

**The more we grow in sensitivity to the Spirit, the fewer mistakes we will make in our decision-making process.**

After a couple of months in Mexico, we were out of money. We were living on pancakes and had to finally drop out of language school. We had no steady support from anyone in the U.S. No church had sent us. We felt as though we were on our own.

In those worsening circumstances, I became very focused on God and began to spend more time in prayer. Something was wrong! In the middle of one of my prayer times, the Spirit of God spoke to me and said, *"What are you doing here, Barry?"* I responded, *"Well, God, you know you've called me to be a missionary; so here I am."* God then went on to teach me the difference between being called and being sent. Because I was a novice at hearing and discerning the voice of God, I had assumed that the call in my heart demanded an immediate action on my part. We only lasted 4 months in Mexico and finally had to return to Texas to begin again. But I had learned a lot!

This is why hearing from God is so vitally important. The more we grow in sensitivity to the Spirit, the fewer mistakes we will make in our decision-making process. Years later, we were sent by God *and* a local church to serve as missionaries in Latin America. We were sent forth with prayer and support. We were visited and counseled. We were not alone this time. We were sent unto the work to which we had been called 11 years earlier.

Whether you know it or not, the Spirit is at work in you.

> *For it is God which worketh in you both to will and to do of his good pleasure.*
>
> *Philippians 2:13*

The urges, tendencies, desires and passions that are alive in you are not there by coincidence. You may not be aware of having heard God concerning your desires and passions in life, but He is working in you. Some of those desires and visions for the future may take time to mature and take shape. The more time you spend in the Word and prayer, the more defined your call and purpose will be. There will probably be months or years of growth and practice involved, but everything God is working in you will come to pass—if you remain sensitive to the Spirit.

> *For we are his workmanship, created in Christ Jesus unto good works, which God hath before ordained that we should walk in them.*
>
> *Ephesians 2:10*

Though today I can say with confidence that I am a teacher in the Body of Christ, I was not always aware of that call nor did I feel particularly equipped for teaching or for anything else, for that matter. I was shy and introverted and something of a loner. My heart was awakened to the possibilities within me on my first mission trip to Mexico while I was a Bible college student in 1977. It was then that the first seeds of a call were sown into my heart, and a desire to effectively communicate the gospel began to grow within me. Just the simple realization that I had something other people needed was a big thing for me. I began to see myself reaching the lost with the gospel.

The desire that was conceived in me didn't come through an audible voice or a verse leaping off the pages of my Bible. It was more of an awareness of a world outside of my own that was needy. Suddenly, I was focused. Though many years passed between the time of that initial awakening and the time of fruitful ministry in

Chile, the call was alive in my heart. I had "heard" God, though I hadn't audibly heard anything at all. The Spirit had quickened my spirit, and my future destiny began to take shape.

Years later I realized our 12 years on the mission field, including 8 years of pastoring, proved to be the preparation time for what I do now. I thought we would live the rest of our lives in Chile, but it turned out to be a season that came to an end so that a new season could begin. As the various seasons of my life have unfolded, I can now look back and see that it was God working in me to will and to do of His good pleasure. I had no idea where He would lead me, but I had a growing idea of what my place in the Body of Christ was to be.

Once I became focused on my future path, other voices lost their influence. Though there were obstacles and bumps in the road, I never lost sight of the seed God had sown in my heart. Hearing Him changed my life.

As I look around at so many fine Christians who seem to be without direction and purpose, it becomes glaringly clear how important it is for each and every one of us to be in communion with God and be sensitive to His leading. A life without purpose will never satisfy.

> *And we know that all things work together for good to them that love God, to them who are the called according to his purpose.*
>
> *Romans 8:28*

Are you called according to His purpose? It doesn't mean you have to see the end from the beginning or that you are fully prepared for every contingency. It simply means that in your fellowship with God, something has been birthed in your heart that ignites your passion, energy and faith. As you remain focused on the thing that burns within you, God causes the periphery circumstances of life to work for your good.

Remember, faith comes by hearing God. You may have faith for something you've never consciously heard God speak to you. But if the faith is there, the hearing took place. The Spirit of God quickened something to your spirit. God is at work in you!

Jesus said to Paul, *"I have appeared unto thee for this purpose."* (Acts 26:16) Though Paul's call to ministry was quite dramatic, the more important aspect of this event is to realize that God also has a purpose for you. No one has been created missing a purpose. Our discovery of that purpose has a lot to do with our ongoing fellowship with the Father.

> *Teach me thy way, O Lord, and lead me in a plain path.*
>
> *Psalm 27:11*

Do you expect to be led by the Spirit? Are you paying attention to the faith that is in you? Are you aware of the opportunities and favor around you? Many times we miss the leading of God because we were expecting something more dramatic or perhaps we weren't expecting anything at all. We wonder why others seem to hear from God when all the while He was trying to break through our own dullness of heart.

Expect to hear from God! It may be an impression. It may be a verse that comes alive to you. It may be an open door of opportunity that ignites your passion. It may be a light bulb moment while listening to a message or during a conversation. It could happen while watching a movie or listening to a song. If your heart is expecting to hear from God, you will. Even during the most mundane activities of life, the Spirit of God is alive and active, and His nature is to reveal things.

> *Incline your ear, and come unto me: hear, and your soul shall live.*
>
> *Isaiah 55:3*

**Beware of playing the "God card."**

I would be remiss to not warn you of something that happens far too often as believers learn to hear from God. How many times have we heard a well-meaning Christian declare that God has told them to do something? Once that declaration has been made, there is no room for correction, further guidance or wise counsel. Many times I have heard such declarations that quite obviously were wrong, but because the person was convinced they had heard from God, they were unwilling to entertain the idea that they could have misinterpreted what they had heard. This had happened to us before our first attempt at being missionaries to Mexico in 1978. We had received counsel that we were getting ahead of God, but I wouldn't listen. I mistook the call for the sending.

In the Kingdom, everything begins with a seed. The seed is not the harvest. We may have the seed of a revelation or the seed of a new direction or the seed of a purpose, but it is important that we give it time to grow and mature. Not every leading of the Spirit or inclination

**God's leadings and direction are fine-tuned through patience.**

of the heart represents the fullness of what God is doing in your life. Give every seed time to mature. Pray over the things you hear the Spirit say.

*But let patience have her perfect work, that ye may be perfect and entire, wanting nothing.*

*James 1:4*

Patience: cheerful endurance.

Patience is powerful. It pays great dividends in life, especially as we learn to hear God and be led by the Spirit. Patience is not to be confused with passivity. The passive have no vision, no goals and no energy. The patient know that the power and promises of God are at work on their behalf, and they cheerfully endure momentary challenges. In the Parable of the Sower, Jesus spoke about the need for patience.

*But the ones (seeds) that fell on the good ground are those who, having heard the word with a noble and good heart, keep it and bear fruit with patience.*

*Luke 8:15 NKJV (parentheses added)*

Fruit is brought forth with patience. God's leadings and direction are fine-tuned through patience. Patience is the constant determination to do the right thing, knowing that spiritual forces are at work on your behalf. The farmer is patient knowing that he has sown good seed, and a good crop WILL come up. *"Behold, the husbandman waits for the precious fruit of the earth, and has long patience for it."* (James 5:7)

The patient are not shaken during adverse circumstances. The patient will prevail. They have created the environment to hear God, and even in those times when the leading is not clear, they continue on in faith and perseverance. They are at peace, knowing that the Word is at work in their circumstances.

> *That ye be not slothful, but followers of them who through faith and patience inherit the promises.*
>
> *Hebrews 6:12*

When we mix faith with patience, we are unstoppable. Our confident expectancy of good, of blessing, favor, divine appointments, open doors, revelation knowledge and health will win the day! In fact, Paul refers to God as "the God of patience!" (Romans 15:5)

Don't jump on the first seeds of a leading and declare to the world that God told you to do something. Allow that seed to grow. Get wise counsel from spiritual, mature friends and leaders. It will save you from possible mistakes and embarrassment.

A true word from God will awaken excitement, vision and faith. If you think you have heard from God and that word produced dread or fear, you should most definitely seek the counsel of those who are more mature in this area. Many times even well-meaning prophets may give words that need some time and seasoning or may need to be put on the shelf. If something doesn't bear witness with your spirit, don't act on it. Pray about it, and wait for it to be quickened to you.

You have a purpose to discover! Expect the Spirit of God to reveal it to you step by step and season by season. It may not be what you envisioned at first, but when you see it, you will rejoice and know that God was at work in you.

> *For ye have need of patience, that, after ye have done the will of God, ye might receive the promise.*
>
> *Hebrews 10:36*

## Chapter Seventeen

# FINAL THOUGHTS

As I have mentioned several times in this book, true faith is spiritual and is a result of spiritual hearing.

> *So then faith cometh by hearing, and hearing by the word of God.*
>
> *Romans 10:17*

Hearing by the Word of God is the first thing (the only thing) that must occur. We must remember that Jesus said His words were Spirit. (John 6:63) It is the Spirit that quickens the spirit of man. "*The Spirit itself beareth witness with our spirit*" (Romans 8:16). Just as Jesus could only do what He heard and saw from the Father, we can only have faith to the degree that God's Word has been quickened to our spirit.

This became real to me in the revelation of righteousness, when I knew I was healed, when I received a word of protection, when I received authority to call my car sold, when I refused the words of the doctor and when I received clear vision for direction in Chile and later in coming to Colorado.

Each and every time that His Word has been quickened to my spirit, faith has been born. Every time I have seen the unseen, faith has been born. I have heard Him during my times of prayer, reading and meditation, and I have heard Him while doing the most mundane chores of life. Creating the environment to hear Him is the key. That environment is nothing more than a seeking, focused heart coupled with a hunger for His Word.

*Blessed is the man that heareth me, watching daily at my gates, waiting at the posts of my doors.*

*Proverbs 8:34*

Without faith, it is impossible to please Him (Hebrews 11:6). In the great chapter 11 of the book of Hebrews, we find a list of the heroes of faith and why they are remembered. In many cases, there was a word from God that motivated them to move into the unseen and do exploits.

Wherever you are right now in your life, you are only one word away from new vision, energy, enthusiasm and faith. God wants to talk to you. Expect to hear Him.

*If any man have ears to hear, let him hear.*

*Mark 7:16*

CALLING
PREPARATION
COMMISSIONING

God is looking for a voice,
Not an Echo.